Worlds in a Box

City Art Centre, Edinburgh

28 May – 16 July 1994

Graves Art Gallery, Sheffield

30 July – 24 September 1994

Sainsbury Centre for Visual Arts,

University of East Anglia, Norwich

10 October – 30 November 1994

Whitechapel Art Gallery, London

9 December 1994 – 12 February 1995

The South Bank Centre

The Art of Communication

BT makes communication possible across the length and breadth of the globe, across time and space.

Working as partners, National Touring Exhibitions and BT help to bring the highest quality art within reach of communities throughout the UK.

National Touring Exhibitions and BT are striving to open new doors and enable even more people to experience art, thereby enhancing both verbal and visual communication.

NATIONAL TOURING *Sponsored by* **EXHIBITIONS BT**
ORGANISED BY THE SOUTH BANK CENTRE
FOR THE ARTS COUNCIL OF GREAT BRITAIN

Acknowledgments

It has taken over two years to put together the exhibition Worlds in a Box. It would not have been possible to mount a touring exhibition of this kind, containing works of great fragility, without the support and faith a large number of artists, individuals and institutions. We are deeply indebted to them all for their contributions both to the exhibition itself and to this catalogue:

Richard. M. Ader, The Joseph and Robert Cornell Memorial Foundation; Monsieur Arman and Mrs Corice-Canton Arman; Clive Barker; Mary Bauermeister; Timothy Baum; Tony Berlant; Marinus and Maria-Rosa Boezem; Angel Bofarull; Madame Danielle Boile; Paul Bonaventura; Dr. Gaby Bosch, Schömer Collection, Austria; Derek Boshier; Maria Gilissen Broodthaers; Jim Buckley; Tom Buckley; Mark King and the Hayward Gallery technicians; Henry Buhl; James Burbidge; Dominique Bürgi; Monsieur César and Pascale Dayaut; William Christenberry; Jeffrey Dennis; Steve Dilworth; Anthony Earnshaw; Jane and Peter England, England & Co.; Amanda Farr, City Arts Centre, Edinburgh; Marcel Fleiss, Galerie 1900-2000, Paris; René Gimpel, Gimpel Fils, London; Glasgow Art Gallery and Museum; Adrian Glew, Tate Gallery Archives; Marian Goodman; Francis Graham-Dixon; Dorothy Halic, Gemini Editions, Los Angeles; Richard Hamilton; Judith A. Harney, The Pace Gallery, New York; Jann Haworth; Jon Hendricks and Laurie Steelink, Gilbert and Lila Silverman Fluxus Collection Foundation; George Herms; Susan Hiller; Pierre Huber and Françoise Sunier, Art and Public, Geneva; Cindy Hubert; Inverness Museum and Art Gallery, particularly Catherine Niven; The Janss Trust; William Jeffett, Sainsbury Centre for Visual Arts; Jasper Johns; Isobel Johnstone and Jill Constantine, Arts Council Collection; Jiří Kolář; L.A. Louver Gallery, California, particularly Peter Goulds and Jane Hart; Françoise Lacampagne; Catherine Lampert and James Peto, Whitechapel Art Gallery; Jean-Paul Ledeur; Marco Livingstone for his help in the initial stages of research; Diter and Sigrid Löw; Will Maclean; the Margulies Family Collection; Marcel Mariën; Marlborough Fine Art, particularly Georgia Wagner; Paul Martin; James Mayor, the Mayor Gallery; Andrew Murray; The Netherlands Office for Fine Arts; Marc Nochella, Ronald Feldman Fine Arts Inc.; Avis Newman; Antony Penrose and Michael Sweeney, the Penrose Collection; Monsieur André-François Petit and Madame Rodica Aldoux of the Galerie André-François Petit; David Platzker; Robert Rauschenberg; Patrick Raynaud; Rolf and Doris Renker; Mrs Dagny Runnqvist; Jan Runnqvist, Galerie Bonnier, Geneva; Florence Régnier-Barral; Brian Rice; Larry Rivers; Jenny Blyth, Curator of the Saatchi Collection, London; Arturo Schwarz; The Scottish Arts Council Collection; Madame Natalie Seroussi; Mr Gilbert and Mrs Lila Silverman; the Sonnabend Collection; Doris Stockhausen; Fred Stiven; Lisa-Ann Sugimoto, the Morgan Gallery, Delaware; Sarah Taggart, Jasper Johns Collection; the staff in the Library at the Tate Gallery, London; Mr and Mrs Tieuli; Monsieur Lucien Treillard; Mr Burkhard Wenger; David White, Curator of the Robert Rauschenberg Collection; Stefan van Raay; Sarah Whitfield; The Whitney Museum of American Art, particularly Ellin Burke; Huang Yongping; Mrs Virginia Zabriskie and Heather B. Nevin, Zabriskie Gallery, New York; Johanes Zechner; Krystyna Ziach; and finally those private collectors who wish to remain anonymous.

Henry Meyric Hughes
Director of Exhibitions

Alexandra Noble
Exhibition Curator

Worlds in a Box: An Introduction

It was the boxes of Joseph Cornell (p.22 and 37) which provided the initial motivation when I began to research this exhibition over two years ago. Here was an artist acting as magus, whose small magic boxes holding assemblages evoking nostalgia for both a past age and childlike innocence were like magnets drawing me across large museum galleries into his self-contained, intimate world. Cornell's perfect understanding of the formal and psychological possibilities of the box, induced me to search for other artists who had explored this form. The result is this exhibition which brings together some of the diversity of box works created by artists throughout the 20th century.

A definition of the box is simple enough: a case or receptacle for containing anything. Within the artists' world this definition is expanded and transformed, for here boxes act as repositories for assemblages, chance events, performances, ideologies, dreams and nightmares. The box can be a stage set (*mise-en-boîte* instead of *mise-en-scène*), a convenient method of packaging, a kind of mail art, a reliquary, a boundary between inside and outside, public and private, an extended frame, a joke, a secret, a cabinet of curiosities . . . It is perhaps the simplicity of the box's form and function that makes it so accessible and versatile, capable of holding many different interpretations, that has attracted artists to appropriate it. It is also a form which appears in our daily lives. We all understand what a box is, because most of our man-made environment conforms to its model: fridges, videos, computers, TV ('the box'), radios, microwaves, cupboards, even the houses we occupy. We also classify, store, carry and package all manner of domestic, professional and industrial materials in boxes.

The box is also a significant metaphor in one of the most famous ancient myths: Pandora, a beautiful woman formed from earth and water by Prometheus or Haphaestus and brought to life with fire stolen from the gods. Pandora became the wife of Epimetheus, and was drawn to a forbidden container in which her brother-in-law, Prometheus, had imprisoned all the Spites, which would otherwise curse humankind. We all know Pandora opened the 'box' and unleashed sins and suffering into the world. The myth points out not only the consequences of a choice between happiness and knowledge, but also that the behaviour of Pandora is archetypal – she was unable to resist the mystery held within a closed container. The difference between Pandora's box and those in this exhibition is that the artists wish us to discover their secrets, and that discovery (with perhaps the exception of Lucas Samaras' *Room No. 3*, p.79) does not wreak dire consequences.

The fascination that artists have shown for this form is, to some extent, inseparable from the histories of assemblage and collage, for art in boxes is a hybrid genre combining painting, printmaking, photography, collage, sculpture and assemblage to create new modes of expression. It is with assemblage, where the constitutent elements are not carved, modelled or drawn, but taken from preexisting manufactured or found materials and objects, that the box most readily adapts itself; three-dimensional configurations often need a structure which acts as container, boundary and protection. . Assemblage extends the traditional idea of composition in two dimensions, i.e. on a picture plane, to arranging elements physically — these arrangements are not merely *ad hoc*, but illustrate the complex, transformative process by which an artist realises his ideas. In a sense there is a contradiction inherent in a boxed assemblage. The construction and juxtaposition of unlikely elements points to a fluid, experimental understanding of the nature of art, whereas the box is a particularly controlled and self-referential structure. However, it is perhaps this contradiction, or tension of opposites, that makes for so many successful experiments in this area (for two very different examples see p.28 and 43).

It was the avant-garde movements of Dadaism and Surrealism, particularly the artists Marcel Duchamp (p.25) and Kurt Schwitters (p.80) and the influential writings of André Breton, that have had such an important bearing on subsequent artists using the box form. Dadaism, founded in Switzerland in 1916, was an international movement of artists who were anarchic and iconoclastic and indulged in shock tactics designed to outrage the conservative cultural standards of the day. Artists such as Laszlo Moholy-Nagy, Hannah Höch and Kurt Schwitters eschewed traditional methods, preferring to use everyday materials – photographs, reproductions from magazines and ordinary printed ephemera in their work. Schwitters embraced junk; his *Merzbau* (aka *Cathedral of Erotic Misery*) was a giant, abstract assemblage made from a chaotic heap of junk materials. It was a vast repository of ideas, reflecting Schwitters attitude towards blending life and art, and contained secret openings and doors hidden within the sprawling structure. It presented an interesting continuum of box forms: those inside the *Merzbau* itself, within two other forms of enclosure, the rooms of his house and the house itself. The *Merzbau* became more Constructivist as it developed over the two decades it took to complete. Even though it was destroyed in 1943, it exists in photographs and has been particularly influential on artists using more architectural and environmental assemblage techniques, notably Louise Nevelson (p.66).

Kurt Schwitters
Merz Construction (Merzbau)
c.1923-33
Assemblage in the artist's home, Hanover, Germany destroyed in 1943.
© DACS 1994

The influence of Dadaist aesthetics re-surfaced in the late 1950s and early 1960s with the renewed interest that artists had in assemblage as an art form and the new junk culture. Certainly Dadaist ideas are prevalent in the works of the *Nouveaux Réalistes*, whose central motif was the mass-produced object (see Arman, p.8 and 34; César, p.19 and Martial Raysse, p.74) and those artists associated with the Fluxus movement (p.30). Marcel Duchamp, also associated with Dadaism, brought all mundane objects into the realm of art, by the act of signing them. Suddenly bicycle wheels, bottle racks and urinals achieved a hitherto unknown *cachet* – these 'Readymades' were to be perceived as art. Certainly 50 years later the legacy of Duchamp acquired an energetic new lease of life through the *Nouveaux Réalistes*.

Duchamp's ground-breaking concept, the *Boîte en Valise*, presents a box as 'museum' enclosed in a travelling case, much in the manner of the collected wares of a travelling salesman. However, it

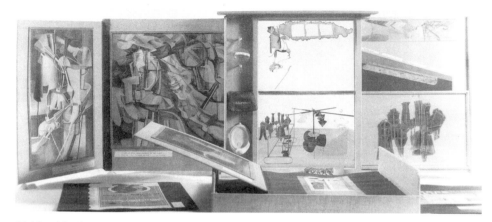

51. Marcel Duchamp
Boîte en Valise (Series C) 1941
linen covered box, lined
with grey-blue Ingres paper
containing 68 items
9 x 38 x 40 cm
· Private collection
© ADAGP, Paris & DACS, London 1994

is a museum of the artist's work which is replicated 300 times. The idea that an artist could assemble a contained collection of his work in this way was further explored in the 1960s in Ben Vautier's *Cupboard* of 1967 (Musée National d'Art Moderne, Centre Georges Pompidou) (see also p.82), Robert Filliou's *Galerie Légitime* (p.29) and Herbert Distel's *Museum of Drawers*, shown at the ICA, London in 1979. The *Boîte en Valise* is the first, complex, multiple edition work of art, pre-dating all the Fluxus boxed collections and Wallace Berman's *Semina Suitcase* containing journals of his writings (p.12). The *Valise* challenged the notion that a work of art must be a unique creation, well before the 1960s explosion of multiple editions (many conveniently packaged in box form, for examples see Beuys p.13, Hamilton p.31 and Man Ray p.54) which were either a reflection of the artist's desire (Beuys, Hamilton) to have an accessible form of artistic exchange or were a more commercial venture based on the status attached to a particular artist's reputation (Man Ray).

Surrealism, born partly out of the demise of Dada in 1922, sought through what Breton described as 'pure psychic automatism' to free artists from conventional pictorial ideas and all previously accepted forms of expression, believing that true reality was only found through alogical insights into the unconscious mind. The artistic manifestations of such thinking produced paintings of highly stylised dreamscapes, automatic drawings and random assemblages of distorted or unexpected objects in bizarre juxtapositions, perfectly summed up in Lautréamont's simile from Malador, 'Beautiful as the chance encounter of a sewing machine and an umbrella on an operating table'. It is this ethos which, in various ways, informs the work of many artists in this exhibition: Eileen Agar, Anthony Earnshaw, Georges Hugnet, Man Ray, Marcel Mariën, Meret Oppenheim and Mimi Parent. The role of the box here is to mostly act as a window onto an unusual world, defining the boundary between the experience of the 'dream' and the outer world of 'reality' that the viewer occupies.

The proliferation of art in boxes during the 1960s was, to a large extent, a result of the socio-economic environment – the post-war consumer boom where goods were subject to all kinds of wrapping, packaging and boxing – and the position of art within a rapidly growing commercial market of exchange. That artists adopted different strategies to counteract the perceived commodification of art is well documented; the most extreme example perhaps was the canning of his own excrement by the Italian artist, Piero Manzoni. However, it was the Fluxus Collective (p.30) which produced works of the greatest – almost overwhelming – variety. The Fluxus box (read activity or game kit) contained assortments of assembled Readymades. This form was to become the mainstay of Fluxus vocabulary and with it Duchamp's legacy held within his *Boîte-en-Valise* came to be fully understood and exploited. Fluxus emerged as distinctly different from the Pop Art movement with which it is often associated, because, unlike the latter, it did not produce works that mirrored the prevailing consumer icons: Coke bottles, Campbells soup cans, Brillo boxes and Camel cigarette packets.

Subsequent developments owe much to these historical impulses. However it would be erroneous to categorise an enormous diversity of practices, since contemporary artists follow their own individual paths and no longer are associated with definable movements or groups. It is through the Artists A – Z in the following pages that individual entries are found. What the artists share is that at some moment in their careers, they came across the box; their investigations have either run parallel to their concerns in other media or are an extension of them. Alternatively, for a specific period they have closely explored the possibilities, structure and form of the box, only to move on later into another field of investigation.

Perhaps the supreme irony in presenting the works in this exhibition is that modern methods of museum display dictate that the experience of viewing these works will mostly be mediated through vitrines – the artist's box is shown in yet another 'box', in a larger rectangle or cube within the 'house' that is the art centre, gallery or museum.

Alexandra Noble
April 1994

Eileen Agar 1904-1991

Eileen Agar attended the Slade School of Art in 1925-26 and then studied in Paris 1928-30. She first saw a Surrealist art work in 1929 and met the poet Paul Eluard at this time. Herbert Read and Roland Penrose, whom she met through the painter, Paul Nash, selected her work for the 1936 Surrealist Exhibition at the New Burlington Galleries, London. Nash influenced her work by his emotional identification with the forms and feelings of nature and his painterly evocations of 'a spirit of place'. Nash's views led Agar to her animistic view of nature, 'Surrealism for me draws its inspiration from nature . . . you see the shape of a tree, the way a pebble falls or is formed, and you are astonished to discover that dumb nature makes an effort to speak to you, to give you a sign, to warn you, to symbolise your innermost thoughts'.[1]

In the summer of 1935 Nash and Agar stayed close by on the Dorset coast. He would bring her curious stones collected on beach walks, which led her to adapting shells and driftwood into strange marine objects and collages. She gathered further materials in the mid-1930s on visits to the beaches of Brittany and Southern France. Agar linked her references to the natural world with those from past civilisations. Here (p.36) the sea-horse and coral are combined with the all-seeing eye of the Egyptian god, Horus, who was the patron of music and art and all things beautiful.

Arman b.1928

Arman (born Armand Fernandez) was one of the founding members of the *Nouveaux Réalistes* in 1960. His work in the 1950s moved through particular phases from *Cachets*, sheets of paper covered with multiple imprints made by a rubber stamp, to *Allure d'objets*, which used other types of inked objects in formal repetition. By 1959 Arman concentrated on boxed accumulations of the same object (see p 34). These ranged from radio lamps, gasmasks, cutlery, spare parts for cars, to alarm clocks, dolls – anything man-made that could be bought in quantity, possessed a strong formal identity and could arrange itself visually. Arman has said, 'I didn't discover the principle of accumulation, it discovered me . . . society feeds its sense of security with a pack-rat instinct demonstrated in its window displays, its assembly lines, its garbage piles. As a witness of my society, I have always been very much involved in the pseudo-biological cycle of production, consumption and destruction. . . . I have been anguished by the fact that one of the most conspicuous material results is the flooding of our world with junk and rejected . . . objects'.[2]

2. Arman
Full Up 1960
sardine tin (with dust and key enclosed)
10.5 x 6 x 3cm
Paul Martin
© ADAGP, Paris & DACS, London 1994

Accumulations dating from 1960, while Arman still lived in Paris, tended to contain used and domestic items, whereas after he settled in New York from 1964, his materials were more industrial. Other accumulations of dolls in boxes include *Massacre of the Innocents* 1961 (Kaiser Wilhelm Museum Krefeld) and *Birth Control* 1963. Arman also used quantities of dolls' eyes and dismembered hands to great effect.

Yves Klein, Arman's friend and collaborator presented *Le Vide (The Void)* at Iris Clert's Gallery in April 1958. Arman conceived *Le Plein (Full Up)* as a physical counterpart to Klein's metaphysical exhibition. It took Arman until 1960 to persuade Iris Clert to allow him to use the gallery as a dumping ground for tons of rubbish. The exhibition was best seen from the outside: what was on show was the gallery itself, not the junk. All that remains of that ground-breaking show is photographic documentation and the boxed invitation card seen here.

4. Ay-O
Tactile Box 1963
cardboard box stamped with
hole in top
31 x 31 x 31.5cm
The Gilbert and Lila Silverman
Fluxus Collection, Detroit

Ay-O b.1931

Ay-O studied in the Fine Arts Division of Tokyo Educational University. He moved to New York in 1958. He met George Maciunas in 1961 and by the end of 1962 was taking part in many Fluxus 'Happenings'. The numerous tactile and finger boxes Ay-O conceived are all variations of a single concept: by sticking your finger through a hole you entered an unknown tactile universe. This idea was further extended in the Fluxus Collective work *Fluxlabyrinth* shown at the 26th Berlin Arts Festival in 1976. Ay-O made *Tactile Entrance*: people were meant to thrust themselves through the entrance consisting of a foam mattress bent into a U-shape. Sexual readings of these works are probably intended. Since 1970 Ay-O has divided his time between Japan and New York.

(see also *Fluxus Collective* p.30)

Clive Barker b.1940

In the 1960s Clive Barker's re-making of popular icons, such as Coke bottles in bronze or chrome, led him to be associated with the Pop Art movement, although he prefers not to be classified in this way. His early work of this period is said to reflect his experience of working on an assembly line at Vauxhall Motors, particularly the use of leather and chrome in his sculptures.

Zip Box No. 1 is the first of three similar works. The inspiration for the work is two-fold. Clive Barker is very keen on leather and had seen Richard Smith wearing a brown leather jacket which became the subject of one of his painting/assemblages entitled *Dick's Jacket 1963*. It was also the centenary year of the zip.

Clive Barker had the idea of asking twelve artists whom he admired to burn their paintings so that he could make a series of new works. Richard Hamilton, David Hockney and Joe Tilson all agreed. Francis Bacon was approached and in principle had no objection, providing Henry Moore burnt one of his drawings, although he felt it was a 'very American idea'; Barker wanted to make an exhibition of twelve works in total. He witnessed the burning of the Hockney painting whose ashes were transferred to a wooden casket. The project was abandoned because the 'performance' involved in the burning of these paintings was not part of his original intention.

7. Clive Barker
Cremated Richard Hamilton Painting 1971
wood casket & ashes
17.5 x 25.2 x 21.7 cm
The artist

10. Mary Bauermeister
Pyramid 1977
glass, ink, wood & sand
60 x 60 x 60 cm
Doris Stockhausen, Cologne

Mary Bauermeister b.1934

During the 1960s Mary Bauermeister made boxes filled with different density lenses and glass balls, using light in the same way that some artists use colour. The works were informed by Bauermeister's studies into systems of numerology, the science of light, crystallography and astronomy. In 1961 Bauermeister studied with the composer, Karlheinz Stockhausen (whom she later married) and subsequently applied techniques of serial music to some of her constructions.

The three examples in this exhibition consist of a wall-mounted box embedded in a linen frame, a look-through and a pyramid box. Although the physical structures may vary, lenses and balls are suspended on different planes, so that light is constantly reflected and when it refracts it leaves coloured outlines on the surfaces of adjoining lenses. The artist seems to want to free scale from a rational idea about space, mirroring the shifting nature of visual perception. Bauermeister also writes words on the glass panes, on the glass spheres, even on the sides of the box. There are messages, warnings and admonitions in these boxes — a three-dimensional word play, not a linear narrative.

Tony Berlant b.1941

Tony Berlant studied at the University of California, Los Angeles. He first showed his 'houses' in the *Boxes* exhibition at the Dwan Gallery, Los Angeles in 1964. Some of his most ambitious sculptures in the 1960s were made for an exhibition *The Marriage of New York and Athens*: large building-like structures based on a combination of the architecture of a skyscraper and a Greek temple. The use of stainless steel on plywood has existed in Berlant's work since this time. Berlant also 'paints' by collaging pieces of tin, both found and fabricated, onto plywood and fixing them with steel brads onto a flat surface. The 'houses', like *Luchita* (p.39), which use the same materials can be equated with the act of 'drawing'; the edges present in the structures are a way 'to challenge and re-investigate the boundaries of the physical object. This in turn informs the picture-ground relationship that exists in the two-dimensional work.'[3]

12. Wallace Berman
Semina suitcase c. 1960
metal suitcase with collaged photographs
20.3 x 25.4 x 9.6 cm
Shirley Berman, Los Angeles
Courtesy L.A. Louver Gallery,
Venice, California

Wallace Berman 1926-1976

The work of Wallace Berman reflects the hybrid nature of the West Coast arts scene in the 1950s, where a crossover between film, music, poetry and visual arts was quite usual (what is now known as the Beat Generation). Wallace Berman exerted an undeniable influence in his lifetime (since his death this has grown to mythic proportions) but his public presence was minimal; he exhibited once at the Feres Gallery in 1957. The content of the exhibition was misunderstood by the authorities and Berman was arrested and convicted of pornography.

His earliest drawings were of jazz musicians in the late 1940s. He then made a series of 'parchments': wood-stained paper with ink drawings of Hebrew letters. These works dealt in codes belonging to the Kabbalah; according to this Jewish mystical tradition God created the universe through the 22 letters of the Hebrew alphabet. A development from this was the painting of rocks with random Hebrew letters; the rocks were sometimes chained to a pedestal or boxed. He also made sculptures (now destroyed) during the 1950s, three were shown in the Feres Gallery in 1957; these held containers for souvenirs or mementos. Each has been described as a kind of reliquary. Pages from *Semina*, the poetry journal which Berman created in 1955 and produced in nine editions of no more than 200 copies until 1964, were also present in these sculptures. The journal, 'a loose-leaf collage', each portfolio painstakingly made by hand, was mailed to friends. Copies were a gift, not available through subscription, and deliberately stood outside the prevailing 1950s American preoccupations with the marketing and selling of everything as a commodity. Here a facsimile set of journals are housed in a travelling case much in the same spirit as Duchamp's *Boîte en Valise* (p. 6).

Joseph Beuys 1921-1986

'My objects are to be seen as stimulants for the transformation of the idea of sculpture . . . or of art in general. They should provoke thoughts about what sculpture can be and how the concept of sculpting can be extended to the invisible materials used by everyone . . . That is why the nature of my sculpture is not fixed and finished. Processes continue in most of them: chemical reactions, fermentations, colour changes, decay, drying up. Everything is in a STATE OF CHANGE.'[4]

Joseph Beuys is acknowledged as one of the most important artists to emerge in the post-war era. He was also a teacher and political philosopher who appealed for democratic anarchy and whose credo 'Every man is an artist' had a profound influence. The works exhibited are from Beuys' large production of multiples; he made 400 between 1965 and 1985. His production differs from other artists because his range of subjects was so much broader, incorporating printed graphics and multiple objects and also records, cassettes, video-tapes, postcards or any combination of materials. In short, multiples promoted Beuys' idea of an extended concept of art. Beuys said, 'I search for a suitable quality in an object which permits multiplication, for instance the quality implying a series, found in this bottle of tonic water (Evervess) . . . just by being an article of commerce this bottle can communicate much through repetition . . . one person says: Yes I've got such a bottle. Another one has such a wooden box and a third one says: I've heard something about political activities, and so all sorts of different concepts converge, and that is what I'm interested in ... the distribution of physical vehicles in the form of editions, because I'm interested in the spreading of ideas.'[5]

16. Joseph Beuys
Bruno Cora Tea 1975
bottle & herb tea, leaded top,
printed label in glazed wood box
28.5 x 11 x 10.5 cm
Ronald Feldman Fine Arts, New York
© DACS 1994

17. Marinus Boezem
Della Scultura e La Luce 1985
mixed media
65 (diameter) x 9 cm
Rijksdienst Beeldende Kunst,
Holland

Marinus Boezem b.1934

Along with Ger van Elk and Jan Dibbets, Marinus Boezem has been
described as one of 'the three musketeers of conceptual art in the
Netherlands'.[6] For Boezem the whole world can be appropriated in
sculptural form. In 1960 he exhibited part of a Dutch polder, in 1963
he discovered air as a sculptural material, and by 1969 he had
signed the sky over the port of Amsterdam by aeroplane using the
jet stream to form his surname. Whether his materials are ready
made or found in nature, themes concerning flight, weather and
mapping occur throughout his career. *Della Scultura e La Luce*, one
of the few works Boezem has made in a box, presents a synthesis
of some of his ideas. Inside a sweet box is an Alpine relief map,
with the lid containing the constellations of the night sky.

Angel Bofarull b.1957

Angel Bofarull studied art history and is self-taught as an artist,
having his first one-person show in 1985. Bofarull makes collages
and objects, some contained within boxes. From childhood he has
sought refuge in the past, consequently his work can evoke feelings
of sadness, solitude and nostalgia and is connected by his wish to

create an intimate world far from present day concerns. Bofarull used to write prose poetry and describes his work as literary, 'writing poetry without writing'.[7]

(see p. 35)

Derek Boshier b.1937

Derek Boshier studied at the Royal College of Art together with Patrick Caulfield, Allen Jones and R.B. Kitaj, among others; he was one of the core members of the British Pop Art movement in the early 1960s when *Marshal* was made, but his involvement was short-lived. The marshal has a target for a head, perhaps an iconographic reference to the Target paintings of Jasper Johns from the mid-1950s (in 1960 Niki de Saint Phalle started a series of assemblages of human figures with dartboard heads) or an ironic commentary that a marshal is always target practice for some gun-slinger. *Marshal* has something in common with Boshier's paintings of this period which showed an acute awareness of the many manifestations of Americana in everyday British post-war life.

19. Derek Boshier
Marshal 1961
mixed media in box
50.8 x 40.6 x 10.1 cm
Brian Rice Collection

George Brecht b.1925

Brecht studied at the Philadelphia College of Pharmacy and Science and then at the New York School for Social Research where he studied musical composition with John Cage. The latter's influence changed the direction of Brecht's art so that he took part in events and performance pieces which led to his association with Fluxus. From 1965-68 Brecht ran a shop, *La Cédille Qui Sourit*, with Robert Filliou (p. 29) in Villefranche-sur-Mer which sold Fluxus works. He was a central figure in Fluxus until its disintegration in 1978.

Water Yam is also referred to as *The Complete Works of George Brecht 1959-1961*. La Monte Young's *Compositions* and *Water Yam* are the first collections of Fluxus works. Many of the cards published are from events and performance pieces that Brecht took part in from 1959. Some were performed at Fluxus concerts. Ben Vautier wrote in 1976, '. . . the most important box is *Water Yam*, for me it is one of the most essential works in the history of art after Marcel Duchamp's bottle rack.'[8]

The contents of *Deck A Flux Game* 1966-67 were produced by a commercial card company for Fluxus. Certain motifs from the cards make up the background for *Universal Machine*.[9]

The series of *Games and Puzzles* came in many variations including ball, bread and bead puzzles; *Valoche/A Travel Aid* was originally listed as part of this series. The work has been described as

21. George Brecht
Water Yam (events) 1959-66
printed cards in plastic box
13 x 18 x 3 cm
Arts Council Collection, South Bank
Centre, London

23. George Brecht
Games and puzzles/
Name Kit 1965-77
mixed media in plastic box
9.3 x 12 x 1.8 cm
The Gilbert and Lila Silverman
Fluxus Collection, Detroit

evoking 'both childhood (a box of toys) and death (a case of objects to begin the after life with).'[10]

(see also *Fluxus Collective* p.30)

Marcel Broodthaers 1924-1976

Marcel Broodthaers was born in Brussels and until the age of 40 he had studied chemistry, worked for a bank, been a book dealer, a film-maker and a poet. Broodthaers was on the fringes of artistic circles in Belgium when he decided to become an artist in 1964. The remaining 12 years of his life were a period of great activity when he made art out of objects, books, words, paint, film, places and photographs. Motifs which recur regularly throughout his work are eggshells and stencilled letters. His first exhibition showed works with the former and mussel shells inside containers or stuck onto other objects. Many artists associated with Pop Art and Fluxus brought the imagery of mass consumption into a fine art context, but Broodthaers brought imagery that had associations with food and wine but also a literary 'high culture' imbued with a rigorous, conceptual orientation. Although some of his objects are 'found', their selection depended on their aesthetic appeal rather than acting as a mundane reflection of daily life. For Broodthaers the box form recurred consistently within his work, whether as cartons for broken egg shells; Laughing Cow boxes; suitcases titled *Sculpture, Chabron* or *Erasmus*, containing bricks, coal and maps; or even an imaginary mortuary room with a coffin containing shelves on which were glass vessels enclosing photographs of his dead friend, the poet, Marcel Lecomte. It is possible that Broodthaers returned to this form repeatedly because the circumscribed boundaries of an enclosed space perfectly defined the given limits of any one of his particular ideas.

29. Marcel Broodthaers
Box with checkerboard design & letters of the alphabet 1975
wood, paper, painting
21 x 24.5 x 5 cm
Private collection

31. Jim Buckley
Hasp 1990
galvanised steel, lead,
plywood & pop rivets
34 x 23 x 15 cm
The artist

Jim Buckley b.1952

Jim Buckley studied at the Crawford School of Art and moved to Glasgow in 1988, where he now lives and works. Before he began making a series of boxes in 1990, Buckley was more concerned with abstract metal sculpture. Some, like *Colony*, are illuminated – the slit inviting the viewer to look inside at an interior architectural space, constructed by melted lead dripped onto metal gauze. Buckley is interested in the relationship between inside and outside.[11] His chosen materials – steel and lead stamped with rivets – are deliberately forbidding, the outside refusing to give information, like metal fortresses closed against the world. This is particularly true of *Hasp* which was one of the first box structures he made. It is a strong box, defending an inaccessible interior, whose contents we can only guess at.

32. James Burbidge
Echo 1991
wood, resin, bitumen/rubber
compound, treated lead foil,
lead sheet, papier mâché,
paint & glass
30.8 x 53.2 x 21.6 cm
Private collection, England & Co.
Gallery, London

James Burbidge b.1959

James Burbidge studied at West Surrey College of Art and Design. The year 1988-89 was a period of intense experimentation for him; concurrent with making floor-based, patinated, ceramic sculpture, he was also working on mixed media and sound installations. It was during this period that he discovered lead foil as a material, which led him to explore lining box structures with it and constructing sculptural elements to place inside. The effect is one of open-ended narratives, held by the privacy of their respective containers. From 1989-93 he made over thirty works using the box form but feels, at present, that he has exhausted its formal possibilities.

César b.1921

César (Baldaccini) attended night-classes at the École des Beaux-Arts in Marseilles, before going to the École des Beaux-Arts in Paris from 1943-48. César had a standard academic training of life classes, wood carving and modelling. By chance, in 1952, he started working with scrap iron, experimenting with various techniques using oxyacetylene and arc welding. By 1956 he had established himself as a master in metal sculpture; he could work with any metal and subject it to his will. He was one of the *Nouveaux Réalistes*, along with Arman (p.8) and Martial Raysse (p.74).

34. César
Container Expansion 1969
printed label, tin containing polyurethane/Freon mixture & pigment
17 x 10 cm in diameter
The artist
© ADAGP, Paris & DACS, London 1994

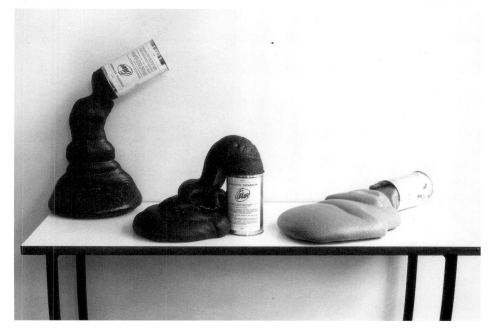

In 1960 the trajectory of César's career radically changed when he exhibited three automobile compressions. César had selected these from the latest model of metal press at a scrap metal factory outside Paris. The press could crush different sizes and weights of metal and César chose the most aesthetic as his own sculptures. This act was a landmark in the history of metal sculpture. Until 1963 he continued to use the technique but then abandoned it; after 1968 he took up compressions again but used different materials, embarking on a series of mini compressions of more domestic objects: for example, *Compression* 1975 is a series of crushed cardboard boxes.

A counterpoint to the idea of compression was that of expansion. César made his expansions in the late 1960s using liquid polyurethane, pigment and an accelerating agent. *Container Expansion* is a multiple edition do-it-yourself expansion kit. By opening the can and mixing the contents the owner can make their own 'Happening'. César travelled extensively between 1967-70 mounting *Expansion Happenings*. A well documented example was one at the Tate Gallery, London in 1968. César also developed combustions, compositions of matchboxes burnt and glued to a flat surface.

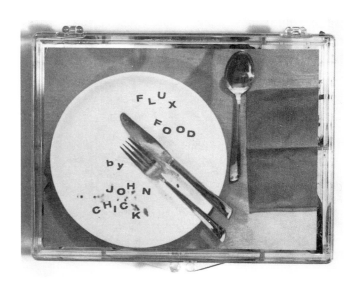

35. John Chick
Flux Food (forest and synthetic) 1968
mixed media in plastic box
9.3 x 12 x 2.6 cm each
The Gilbert and Lila Silverman
Fluxus Collection, Detroit

John Chick

The only official Fluxus work to go out under the artist's name was *Fluxfood. Fluxfood* was a much varied edition. George Maciunas (p.51) designed two different labels and the contents differed from box to box. *Synthetic Food* consisted of styrofoam pieces, while *Forest Food* could contain lichens, acorns, pine needles etc.[12]

(see also *Fluxus Collective* p.30)

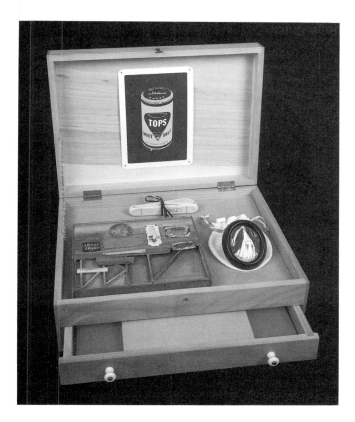

39. William Christenberry
The Alabama Box 1980
mixed media
15.5 x 45 x 31.4 cm
The artist

William Christenberry b.1936

Christenberry's work encompasses painting, sculpture, photography, drawing and installation, but all of it is rooted in his recollections of his Alabama childhood. Even though Christenberry has lived in Washington D.C. since 1968, he returns to Hale County, Alabama every year. In 1973 he made boxes from pieces of wood found in that rural landscape, which were intended to be crude and clumsy. Although Christenberry eventually destroyed these works he came to see them as pivotal. Certainly his series of *Building Constructions* – small-scale recreations of barns and churches – inspired by his Alabama landscape photographs and his *Dream Buildings* suggest sophisticated box structures.

Alabama Box, with its found objects, a relief sculpture, ten photographs and soil, shows Christenberry's deep preoccupation with the experience of living in the American South.

Klan Dolls (p. 62) is one example of a huge body of work that Christenberry has constructed since the 1960s. He made *Klan*

Room in 1975, which is a multi-media environment about the activities of the Klu Klux Klan. The accuracy of the works Christenberry made, particularly the details on the costumes of the Klan dolls, are from his recollections of Klan rallies he attended in the 1960s. This vast work has caused much controversy; a burglary in his studio in 1979 resulted in most of the Klan Room being stolen. Christenberry has since reconstructed it on three times the scale. Christenberry is vehemently opposed to the Klan and his work has been described as a 'kind of exorcism of racism'.[13] The Klan Dolls are bound and boxed, perhaps to contain their pernicious evil, much as the Spites and Furies unleashed by the mythical Pandora were once safely contained in a jar.

Joseph Cornell 1903-1972

Joseph Cornell lived with his mother and brother, Robert, who suffered from cerebral palsy, in Queens, New York. His beginnings in art were through making toy-like objects for his brother's amusement. Cornell was a great bibliophile and was familiar with the early collage-novel of Max Ernst, La Femme 100 Têtes; certainly his early collages show the influence of Ernst. From 1921 Cornell worked for a wholesale textile company, but he lost his job in 1931. With more spare time he discovered the Julien Levy Gallery in Manhattan where he came into contact with works by European Surrealists among others. Manhattan was as far as he ever travelled; he liked nothing better than to scavenge in the souvenir shops off Times Square and to go through back numbers of old magazines. Cornell had a nostalgia for the ephemera of a past age; he was particularly fond of Victoriana – toys and stuffed animals under bell jars. He exhibited at the Julien Levy Gallery throughout the 1930s and also in some of the famous international Surrealist exhibitions of that time. By 1940 his career as an artist was assured. He made hundreds of boxes until the end of the 1950s when the difficulty in obtaining his preferred materials meant Cornell's production of boxes declined; he turned more to collage in his later years.

Cornell has erroneously been called a Surrealist, but he did not share André Breton's psychological theories. He was attracted to the Surrealists' visual ideas, particularly their free use of objects. His boxes do not contain unsettling juxtapositions of objects but rather harmonious and poetic assemblages.

Cornell made both sand boxes and fountains. They were designed to be picked up and tilted, so that the sand formed different patterns over the image.

His extensive knowledge of art history came mostly from books and visits to Manhattan's museums. Cornell made a series of works between 1948 and 1954 where a reproduction of Bronzino's Bia di Cosimo de' Medici is the central image (see front cover).

Cornell travelled the length and breadth of Europe in his mind, aided by guidebooks, transport timetables and postcards. He produced many boxes which have some reference to hotels – the hotel being a metaphor for travelling both geographically and historically. Empty hotel boxes could be seen to evoke the loneliness of the traveller.

Bird boxes have great metaphorical significance. His parrots and cockatoos are positive symbols, whereas the owl is a night bird and is often seen as a bird of death in *momento mori*.

(see p.37)

45. Joseph Cornell
Apollinaires 1954
box construction
43.2 x 30.5 x 14 cm
The Joseph and Robert Cornell
Memorial Foundation

48. Jeffrey Dennis
Six Easy Breathers 1991
oil paint on polymerised board
& canvas
150 x 100 x 170 cm
The artist

Jeffrey Dennis b.1958

Jeffrey Dennis studied at the Slade School of Fine Art from 1976-80. He continues to live and work in London. Jeffrey Dennis is not immediately associated with sculpture. He is known as a painter of the cityscape, his truncated narratives reflections of our 'dis-ease' with urban life. In recent years he has been making constructions which have a direct relationship to his paintings and vice versa.

Six Easy Breathers is a collection of boxes connected by a haphazard network of tubing. The surface of the boxes is covered with a kind of painted pebble-dash on which are floated postcard-sized glimpses of everyday city life. Here these vignettes are hidden, only to reveal themselves at unexpected angles as we walk around the sculpture – the experience is of camouflage, but also, in some senses, mirrors the dislocation and confusion experienced in urban life. Paintings like *Box Not Yet Shut* and *News From Nowhere*14 provide, in a configuration of interlocking canvases with painted tubular structures, a two-dimensional approach to similar ideas.

Steve Dilworth b. 1949

Steve Dilworth studied at Maidstone College of Art from 1967-71. His recent sculpture has its origins in the natural cycle of life and death he witnesses along the shoreline at his home on the Isle of Harris in the Outer Hebrides. Nature in the form of dead birds, sand eels, fish and sheep vertebrae are his materials, together with the elements of wood, air and water. *Fish Box* is one of the many caskets or carapaces he has built for dead creatures, the lines of each casket follow the shape of its eventual incumbent. He often describes these as 'travelling' or 'throwing' objects.

49. Steve Dilworth
The Fish Box 1991
driftwood, fish, fishing line, bog oak
25 x 50 cm .
Scottish Arts Council Collection

Marcel Duchamp 1887-1968

Marcel Duchamp was one of the most innovative artists of the 20th century; his ideas have influenced generations of artists. He was born in Blanville, Normandy into a cultured family, his two brothers Jacques Villon and Raymond Duchamp-Villon were both artists. Duchamp's early paintings show he had looked at Cézanne and the Fauves. The discovery of photographs of bodies in movement by Etienne-Jules Marey influenced his *Nude Descending a Staircase* (1912). This painting was the centre of controversy at the New York Armory show in 1913 and by the time Duchamp first arrived in the U.S.A. in 1915, he was already famous. This, combined with his signing of everyday objects as art assured his position as a leading member of the avant-garde. From 1923 Duchamp encouraged the fiction that he no longer made art but had decided to concentrate on playing chess instead.

In 1934 he published *The Green Box* (its contents date from 1911-15) in an edition of 300; these contained facsimiles of notes and drawings which related to the making of *The Bride Stripped Bare by Her Batchelors, Even*, his huge painting on glass, also referred to as *The Large Glass* (1915-24).

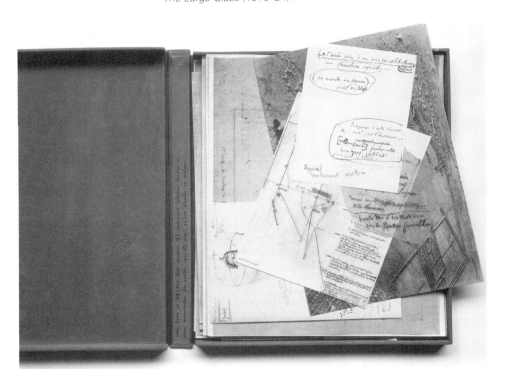

50. Marcel Duchamp
The Green Box 1934
94 documents in a cardboard box covered with flock paper
33 x 28 x 19 cm
Private collection
© ADAGP, Paris & DACS, London 1994

Duchamp said of his *Boîte en Valise* in 1955, '. . . Instead of painting something new, my aim was to reproduce the paintings and objects I liked and collect them in a space as small as possible . . . I first thought of a book, but I did not like the idea. Then it occurred to me that it could be a box in which all my works would be collected and mounted like a small museum, a portable museum, so to speak.'[15] Duchamp first started work on *Boîte en Valise* (p.6) in Paris between 1935-36. Duchamp's idea produced a completely new form of art work, a portable museum of miniature replicas and colour reproductions of his work in a travelling case. He smuggled his materials out of occupied France in 1940, using a cheese merchant's identity card. The first 20 boxes were assembled in New York in 1941; a further 90 were put together during the war years with the help of Joseph Cornell (p.22) among others. 30 further copies, of which this is one example, were assembled in Paris in 1958 by Ilias Zanevitch. No more than 300 copies existed by the time of Duchamp's death in 1968.

Anthony Earnshaw b.1924

Anthony Earnshaw left school in 1939 and for the next 25 years was variously employed in the heavy engineering industry in Leeds as a turner, fitter and crane driver.

He made an important friendship with Eric Thacker in 1941. Through their interest in poetry, particularly the work of Arthur Rimbaud , Earnshaw discovered Surrealism in 1944-45. Whenever he could, he visited the London Gallery, Brook Street, run by the poet E.L.T. Mesens. Earnshaw has said, 'The spell it (Surrealism) then cast remains a frisky imp haunting my life to this day.'[16] His first paintings date from that time. He painted sporadically throughout the 1950s and 1960s. He wrote and illustrated two fantastic novels with Eric Thacker in 1968 and 1971, *Musrum* and *Wintersol.* They also co-devised a cartoon strip, *Wokker,* which was published in *The Times Educational Supplement* in 1971-72. It was not until the mid-1970s that Earnshaw started making boxed assemblages, which are sometimes homages to artists from Surrealism's first wave: Man Ray and André Breton. They are also rooted in an English tradition of social satire and whimsy. Ironies are exposed, but the jokes are never lost.

The Blind Engine Driver is a variation of a box called *The Blind Elephant 1987:* an elephant from a knick-knack shop, its eyes removed, its trunk painted white, its body black, mounted behind smoked glass. Earnshaw alludes to Duchamp's famous *The Bride Stripped Bare by Her Bachelors, Even* which is the subject of the documents contained in *The Green Box* (p.26).

54. Anthony Earnshaw
The Bride with Her Bachelors, Again: after Marcel Duchamp 1991
mixed media
44 x 40 x 10 cm
The artist

Yolande Fièvre 1907-1983

After travelling and living for several years in Egypt during the 1920s, Yoland Fièvre studied at the École des Beaux-Arts in Paris. Subsequently she taught at the École des Beaux-Arts in Orleans. Although no works of hers survive from the 1930s, she was known to have painted in a traditional manner. Her meeting with André Breton and contact with other Surrealists changed the direction of her work. From 1933 until 1967 she made automatic drawings and paintings, mostly 'portraits', influenced by Breton's definition of Surrealism: 'Pure psychic automatism by which one intends to express the real function of thought, be it verbally, in writing, or whatever other manner.'[17]

Fièvre had her first exhibition in 1957 which marked the beginning of her box-reliefs in which she placed flotsam, driftwood and flints found on Normandy beaches. By 1962 these had developed into accumulations of natural objects: bark, bones, root stumps, stones and driftwood. The effect is one of a dynamic, yet controlled, rhythmic ordering of natural forms, both vertically and horizontally. After 1962 the box-reliefs changed, becoming less homogenous with arabesque roots thrusting through the vertical and horizontal divisions. There was more sense of movement; she also introduced coloured woods. After the death of her husband in 1968, she seems to have stopped working, producing little until her death, apart from three exhibitions in 1969, 1973 and 1974.

56. Yolande Fièvre
Refuge pour le Rêve 1968
box relief with wood & stones
35 x 35 x 12 cm
Galerie Natalie Seroussi, Paris

57. Robert Filliou
Flux Hair c.1966
plastic box with hair
12 x 9.3 x 1.3 cm
The Gilbert and Lila Silverman
Fluxus Collection, Detroit

Robert Filliou 1926-1987

Robert Filliou studied economics at U.C.L.A. and subsequently travelled in South Korea, Egypt, Spain and Denmark before settling in France in 1959. Filliou had his first one-man exhibition at the Koepcke Gallery, Copenhagen in 1961 where he showed his first 'wrapped' poems. In 1962 he devised a personal street event, exhibiting works in a hat – the *Galerie Légitime*. This perfomance took place on the streets of Paris, London and Frankfurt. He later developed this idea into a multiple work *Frozen Exhibition* (1972) where a cardboard bowler hat contained a retrospective survey of photographs and texts of Filliou's past performances and exhibitions. Filliou participated in Fluxus events in the 1960s, but not on a regular basis. From 1965-68 he ran *La Cédille Qui Sourit* with George Brecht (p.16).

In 1970 he founded the *Republic Génial*, its purpose to cultivate human genius: 'Basically, I think I am a genius without talent, and if I explain to you what I mean by genius, you will understand my point of view. I think simply that by being a man or a woman, one is a genius, but most people forget it (they are too preoccupied to exploit their talents).'[18]

Filliou made three *Optimistic Boxes*, multiple editions produced by Editions Vice-Versand, Remscheid.

Fluxus Collective

Central to Fluxus' philosophy is the idea of collectivism. George Maciunas, the founder of Fluxus (p. 51) was concerned that Fluxus events, whether they were performances or art works, should not promote the individual ego of any given artist, but should further the collective identity of the movement. Maciunas' ideas were modelled, in part, on Levyi Front Iskusstv – a 1920s Soviet artistic group. It was Maciunas who mostly controlled Fluxus production; he worked collaboratively with artists, realising their ideas, or interpreting them for the best end result. He also oversaw the distribution of editions through mail order, Fluxus newspapers, concerts, *Fluxfests* and artist-run *Fluxshops*. The box was a perfect 'house' for gathering both objects and egos, which could then be subsumed within the identity of the collective work. Collective Fluxus works like the *Year Boxes* and the *Flux Kit* were used as propaganda for the movement. Other collective works, like the *Flux Amusement Center* or the *Flux Labyrinth*, functioned more as interactive environments.

Flux Kit BA 1965 contains work by 13 artists: Eric Andersen, Ay-O, George Brecht, Dick Higgins, Joe Jones, Alison Knowles, Takehisa Kosugi, Nam June Paik, Ben Patterson, Chieko and Mieko Shiomi, Ben Vautier, Robert Watts.

(see p.38)

61. Fluxus Collective
Fluxus Year Box 2 1966-68
wooden box containing
miscellaneous objects
20.3 x 20.3 x 8.6 cm
The Gilbert and Lila Silverman
Fluxus Collection, Detroit
(above, lid; below, contents)

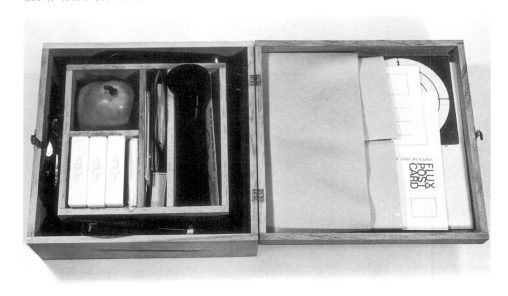

Richard Hamilton b.1922

Richard Hamilton is well known as one of the creators of Pop Art, but since 1964 his work has also addressed social and political issues ranging from the Northern Ireland conflict to the Gulf War; he is also respected as a teacher and writer on art.

The Critic Laughs was originally inspired by a giant set of edible teeth given to the artist by his son. Hamilton stuck the teeth on to his Braun electric toothbrush, and this new 'ready-made' recalled Jasper Johns' sculpture, *The Critic Smiles* (1959), hence the title. In 1971 Hamilton was asked by René Block, the well known collector, gallery owner and publisher, to produce a multiple edition for his Berlin gallery. It was then that the idea to produce *The Critic Laughs* in the style of a mass-produced consumer product arose. Hamilton had asked Hans Sohm (Fluxus collector extraordinaire and dentist) to reproduce the now stickily decomposing teeth in plastic. Braun supplied the mechanical part, and the box aped that of the Braun Sixtant electric razor. The component parts of *The Critic Laughs* deliberately mirrored 1960s mainstream commercial packaging of electrical gadgets. Intentionally, the division between art and life was merged.[19]

62. Richard Hamilton
The Critic Laughs 1968-71
electric toothbrush, false
teeth & container
26.5 x 11 x 6 cm
The artist
© DACS 1994

Jann Haworth b.1942

Jann Haworth studied art at U.C.L.A. from 1959-61 before coming to England to study at the Slade School of Fine Art between 1962-63. She was associated with the Pop Art movement during the 1960s. Her collaboration with Peter Blake on the cover design for the Beatles' *Sergeant Pepper* album cover is perhaps her best-known work. In 1973 she founded the Looking Glass School in Wellow, Avon. She was one of the seven artists, along with Peter Blake, Graham and Annie Ovenden who formed the Brotherhood of Ruralists in 1975. Her work in the 1970s has been described as three-dimensional, magic realism: a world of doll-like, faerie creatures, some enclosed in ornate glass boxes.

The idea for *Richard III* coincided with an invitation to design covers for the New Arden Shakespeare edition: *Richard III, Coriolanus, Macbeth, Henry V* and *Twelfth Night* were Haworth's contribution to the series. The book cover was of a mask made in glass and terracotta. The sculpture is a mirrored box, containing the larger face of Richard III and the smaller faces of the two Princes. Their mouths are opened in a scream, a portent of their tragic fates. The mirrors carry the scream into infinity, enhancing both the psychological power of the sculpture and the wave-like rhythm formed by the porcelain heads.

63. Jann Haworth
Richard III 1980
wood, mirror, porcelain & paint
26.8 x 37 x 27.2 cm
Arts Council Collection, South Bank
Centre, London

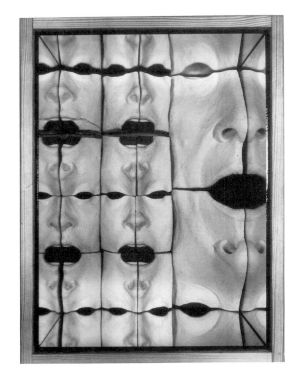

88. Man Ray
Pechage 1969
assemblage with painted
wood box & plastic
36 x 24 x 11.5 cm
Lucien Treillard Collection
© Man Ray Trust/DACS, London 1994

3. Arman
*The Village of the
Damned 1962*
dolls in display vitrine
53 x 51 x 28 cm
Dagny Runnqvist Collection,
Geneva
© ADAGP, Paris & DACS, London 1994

18. Angel Bofarull
Untitled 1990
mixed media
5.5 x 7 x 8 cm
The artist

1. Eileen Agar
Untitled 1936
watercolour, corals, sea horse,
eye of Horus amulet, feather
& lace in a wooden box
15.8 x 22.6 x 5.3 cm
Oliver Murray

46. Joseph Cornell
L'Humeur Vagabonde
c. late 1950s
box construction
17.2 x 19 x 8.2 cm
The Joseph and Robert Cornell
Memorial Foundation

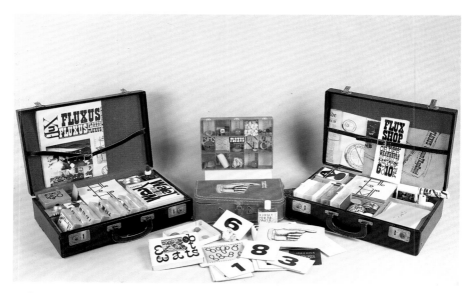

60. Fluxus Collective
Flux Kit (BA copy) 1965
black vinyl attaché case containing
miscellaneous boxed kits
32.5 x 44.5 x 12. 5 cm (closed)
The Gilbert and Lila Silverman
Fluxus Collection, Detroit

11. Tony Berlant
Luchita No. 68 1990
found metal collage on
plywood with steel brads
64.7 x 53.4 x 63.5 cm
L.A. Louver Gallery, Venice,
California

72. Georges Hugnet
Untitled c.' 1936 -37
box with model sailing ship, dice
& collage of women's faces
11.5 x 17 x 4 cm
Timothy Baum, New York

Geoffrey Hendricks b.1931

Geoffrey Hendricks studied at Rutgers University where he met
Robert Watts (p. 84) and Allan Kaprow in 1956. A year later he met
George Brecht (p. 16). Hendricks began to produce paintings using
the sky as subject matter in 1965; he continues to do so to this day.
His most famous work is a sky painting used as the cover of John
Lennon's *Imagine* album.

Flux Reliquary exists in at least three versions: a vending machine
dispensing cat excrement, a seven-part plastic box with relics and
as a drawer of the Fluxus Collective work, *Fluxcabinet*.[20] The work
is perhaps not so much anti-religious as a refreshing exposé of the
hypocrisy surrounding a bogus relics trade. At a *Fluxexhibit* in
Rome, Hendricks said, '. . . you could instal (sic) a few vending
machines which you could obtain locally. One could dispense cat
shit, with the label saying: Fluxrelics, holy shit from the diners of
the Last Supper . . .'[21]

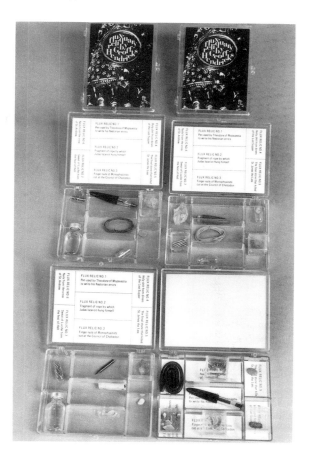

64. Geoffrey Hendricks
Flux Reliquary 1973
plastic box, printed card &
miscellaneous objects
12 x 9.2 2.3 cm
The Gilbert and Lila Silverman
Fluxus Collection, Detroit

66. Maurice Henry
Homage to Paganini 1968
wood, straw & cloth
53 x 26 x 12 cm
Arts Council Collection, South Bank
Centre, London
© ADAGP, Paris & DACS, London 1994

Maurice Henry b.1907

Dada and Surrealism made a profound impression on Maurice
Henry. He met André Breton in 1927 and was to remain in his circle
of followers until 1951, when Henry left after one of his frequent
arguments with Breton. In 1926 Henry formed a group with young
poets and thinkers, called *Le Grand Jeu;* these included Josef Sima
and Roger Gilbert-Lecomte. Henry also founded a review of the
same name in which many of his poems, texts and drawings
appeared. The review folded in 1931. Henry was certainly known
more for his poetic activities; he published five anthologies of
poetry between 1937 and 1969. He also dabbled in journalism and
humorous drawing.

Homage to Paganini was first conceived in 1936 and supposedly
exhibited at the Ratton Gallery, Paris in the same year. This multiple
edition of 25 was published by Sergio Tosi of Milan.

George Herms b.1935

George Herms has been working as an artist since the mid 1950s, when he joined the shifting configuration of artists like Wallace Berman and Artie Richer, poets Robert Alexander, David Meltzer and Cameron, and jazz musicians who made up the Bay Area arts scene. Herms' work over the last 30 years has incorporated performance, film-making and poetry as well as most visual media. He is perhaps best known for his assemblages; the boundaries of this medium were extended and re-vitalised by West Coast artists like Herms, Bruce Conner and Ed Kienholz during the 1960s.

Artie Richer, who died in 1965, was a Beat expressionist painter and friend of George Herms. He was instrumental, along with Wallace Berman (p.12), in Herms becoming an artist. *Drugstore* is a salute to a friend and mentor; it comprises units of shelving, originally bought by Herms from a drugstore in Tustin in Orange County c.1980. These shelves were used as such in Herms' studio until the death of Richer when they became the structure for *Drugstore*. The numerous objects placed in the many box-like compartments are often presents from friends, selected more for their formal qualities than nostalgic associations. *Drugstore for Artie* is but one in a series of celebrations of close friendships made between 1986 and the present: *The Berman Peace* (1986) is another-large scale assemblage – a homage to Wallace Berman.

67. George Herms
Drugstore for Artie 1991-92
mixed media
269.2 x 259 x 91.4 cm
The artist and L.A. Louver Gallery,
Venice, California

Susan Hiller b.1940

Susan Hiller is an artist who was trained in anthropology. It is the dialogue between these two disciplines which gives her work its particularity. Hiller's knowledge of scientific methods of recording information has meant it is easy for her to present her ideas in a wide range of media: painting, sculpture, printed texts, sound and video and large-scale installation – no medium being any more or less important than another.

The three works presented here are part of a larger, ongoing project involving the collection of objects, both found and ready-made, and the process of assembling and classifying materials. Some elements may have been in suspended animation in her studio before finding their way into a particular box. The uniformity of presentation resists any element taking precedence. There is no hierarchy of forms within the boxed presentation, only the juxtaposition of parts transforming the source material: here, elemental forces – Australian earth, obsidian shards, water. As Hiller has said, 'I am only interested in artefacts in so far as they are part of an interrogation and questioning of who I am, who we are and what the making and placement of these artefacts is about'.[22]

69. Susan Hiller
Chamin-Ha (House of Knives) 1992
obsidian projectile points
& photocopy
25.4 x 34.2 x 6.35 cm
Gimpel Fils, London

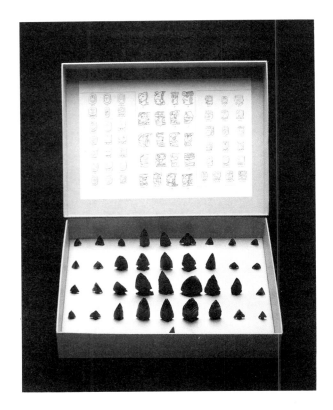

71. Rebecca Horn
*Love Affair Between a
Goose Egg and a Brown
Paper Bag 1990*
glass, steel vitrine, music
sheets, goose egg, paper bag
102.8 x 69.8 x 35.5 cm
Margulies Family Collection

Rebecca Horn b.1944

Whilst a student at the Fine Arts Academy, Hamburg between
1964 - 69, Rebecca Horn contracted lung poisoning. The experience
of that long and debilitating illness has subsequently surfaced
symbolically in her art. One of the central themes in Horn's work is
that of enclosure: from the early body-sculptures (made of cotton,
bandages and feathers) used to cloak the body in her performance
pieces during the 1970s, to some of her large-scale mechanical
objects and vitrine works made in the 1980s and early 1990s. An
example is *The Chinese Fiancée (1976)*, a six-door construction
which encloses the viewer once he or she has stepped onto its
platform, in a space filled with audible Chinese whispers. Such an
enclosure is ambiguous: does it signify safety or entrapment?

Here we have a love affair between a goose egg (perhaps a symbol
of the female: vulnerable, pure and fertile) and a brown paper bag
circumscribed by a steel and glass vitrine. Music (food of love) can
travel through the barrier, but will this love affair wither within the
prescribed confines of its box?

Georges Hugnet 1906-1974

Georges Hugnet spent time in Buenos Aires as a child, returning to Paris in 1913. In 1920 he met Jean Cocteau, Picasso, Marcel Duchamp (p. 25), Max Ernst and Man Ray (p. 54) among others. In 1926 he started to draw in the Surrealist manner. From 1928-32 he collaborated on many periodicals, publishing his first collection of poems, *40 Poésies de Stanislas Boutemer*, in 1928. The following year he founded *Editions de la Montagne* and published books by Tristan Tzara and Gertrude Stein. From 1932-36 he worked on an important study of the Dada movement, *The Spirit of Dada in Painting*, for *Cahiers d'Art*. It was during this period that he was introduced by Tzara to André Breton and entered the Surrealist group but, after a major argument with the latter, he left in 1939.

In the 1930s, Hugnet also made constructions, but these were related to his love of books: his 'reading objects' (*reliures*) set artefacts into recesses within a book's binding. Raymond Roussel's *Locus Solus* had dice, sea shells, a glass eye and a fly placed within the outer cover. He made reading objects of Paul Eluard's *Défense de Savoir*, Hans Bellmer's *La Poupée* and Breton's *L'Air de l'eau*. Motifs from these *reliures* appeared in his assemblages and collages of the period.

(see p.40)

73. Joe Jones
Fluxmusic c.1965
black vinyl attaché case
containing 10 winding devices
32.5 x 44.5 x 12.5 cm
The Gilbert and Lila Silverman
Fluxus Collection, Detroit

Joe Jones b.1934

Joe Jones studied jazz at the Harnett Music School in 1960 and experimental composition with John Cage. In 1963 his work first appeared in an exhibition of toys by artists at the Betty Parsons Gallery, New York. In the mid-1960s he participated in music 'Happenings'.

All works Joe Jones made for Fluxus have a strong musical bias; one of his most ambitious musical machines was the *Mechanical Flux Orchestra* consisting of mechanised violins, bells and aerophones made in 1965.

Fluxmusic is similar to *Electric Music Machine* (aka *Fluxmusic Box* 1965) where 12 music movements were contained in an attaché case, but the elements were automatic, not manual. Jones also conceived *Flux Products of 1961-69*: 12 spring noise makers in an attaché case. All these works are related in their use of hidden musical elements which are operated either electrically or wound up by hand.[23]

74. Per Kirkeby
Solid Plastic in Plastic Box 1967
12 x 9.4 x 1.1 cm
The Gilbert and Lila Silverman
Fluxus Collection, Detroit

Per Kirkeby b.1938

From 1968-74 Kirkeby studied geology at Copenhagen University. Whilst still a student he was experimenting, exhibiting and publishing in a range of art forms including installation, performance and film-making. He had his first one-man exhibition in 1965. Since 1974, Kirkeby has travelled worldwide and developed a considerable reputation as a painter.

Boxed Solids was developed by George Maciunas from an idea by Kirkeby. Kirkeby's suggested prototype was for a metal box containing sawdust with a label 'This box contains wood' and entitled *Fluxwood. Solid Plastic . . .* was the only boxed solid produced as a *Fluxedition* and it had three colour variations: red, black and white. Other materials suggested were clay in a ceramic box and glass, leather, metal and wood in boxes made from the same substances.[24]

Jiří Kolář b.1914

Jiří Kolář is one of the few artists from Middle Europe to achieve an international reputation since 1945. It is perhaps all the more remarkable since he is self-taught as an artist. His first interest was in poetry; seeing a Czech translation of Marinetti's *Parole in Libertá* opened his mind to the possibilities of an innovative use of typography, syntax and layout. This, combined with a love of modern art, led him to exhibit his first collages in 1937, using reproductions of paintings. In 1942 he formed *Group 42* with sculptors, poets, photographers and art historians; their aim was to integrate art into the contemporary life of the metropolis. *Group 42* dispersed with the Communist takeover of Czechoslovakia in 1948. Kolář lost his job as editor in a publishing house, his books were considered subversive and he was tried and sentenced in 1953 to a year's imprisonment. Kolář's interest in collage revived in 1949 and by 1959 he typed out poems without words in free-form arrangements; the transition to visual poems incorporating collage was the next step. In the 1960s Kolář extended the generic term of collage in a wide variety of ways. His *Dictionary of Methods* lists 120 methods of collage he invented. These include the crumpling, tearing up and misapplying of reproductions of paintings, photographs, handwritten or printed texts to flat surfaces or a wide variety of domestic objects.

Nest Box (p. 58) is a superb example of *chiasmage*, where the surface composition is made up of tiny scraps or cut-outs of paper, printed with a chosen text. The composition over the surface of the box is arranged in a variety of patterns, while certain areas are picked out and defined by colour and geometry. The result is that the surface of the box has the appearance of movement. As Kolář has said, 'Chiasmage taught me to see the world and myself from an infinity of viewpoints'.[25]

Kolář was a signatory of *Charter 77* and has lived outside Czechoslovakia since 1979. From 1980 he settled in Paris, and it was not until 1992 that his Czech citizenship was restored.

Françoise Lacampagne b.1943

Since 1979 Françoise Lacampagne's work has combined salvaged wood and stones found on the beaches of the Landes and Basque regions of France. Lacampagne does not collect natural objects at random; each piece has a specific purpose in her work, to reflect a given state of mind, but always one that evokes a love of nature. In any one of her arrangements of elements each part must retain its individual essence as well as working collectively. In the mid-1980s she made a series using drawers to contain and order her experience of the natural world. Now she is making sculptures of stumps and pebbles, allowing the wooden shapes to dictate the form a work might take.

(see p.60)

Nikolaus Lang b.1941

Nikolaus Lang's childhood was spent in Oberammergau, where
there is a strong tradition of woodcarving. His interests were in art,
biology and botany. He went on to study sculpture at the Academy
of Art in Munich from 1960-66. He came to England in 1966-67 as
a postgraduate student at Camberwell School of Art and stayed on
teaching until 1969. Lang was deeply affected by the landscape in
Cornwall and the London parks, particularly Richmond and
Wimbledon Common. He collected objects found on his walks,
preserved them in alcohol and chose perspex boxes in which to
display them. In 1970 he invited 100 people on a 'short walk' on
Wimbledon Common to view found objects in boxes, in locations
where they had originally been discovered by Lang. In 1971-72
Lang went to Japan and extended his practice of collecting and
preserving materials from his walks: these dead insects, birds,
fragments and roots were stored in lacquer boxes named after the
respective landscapes in which they were found. Lang's enduring
preoccupations have been with the balance between nature and
culture. Since 1979 he has spent much time in the Australian
outback.

Untitled c.1970 was a gift to Roland Penrose and Lee Miller. The postcard of David's Napoleon was sent to Lang (he now cannot remember who by) with the request to 'do something with it' and return it; all the re-worked postcards were mounted in an exhibition. As Lang says, 'The work is quite clear – it shows I am not an admirer of Napoleon!'[26]

78. Nikolaus Lang
Untitled c.1970
mixed media assemblage in
perspex box
16.3 x 12.1 x 5.6 cm
Penrose Collection, England

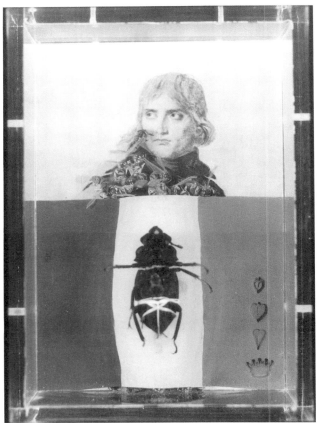

Sol LeWitt b.1928

Sol LeWitt graduated from Syracuse University in 1949. After a tour of duty in Japan and Korea with the U.S. Army he settled in New York in 1953, attending the Cartoonists and Illustrators School. Between 1954-60 he worked on his own paintings and did commercial design work, including graphic and three-dimensional design for architect I.M. Pei on a project for Roosevelt Field Shopping Center, Long Island (1955-56). From 1960-65 he worked at the Information/Book Sales Desk of the Museum of Modern Art, New York and was also night receptionist for the Museum's school, The People's Center.

It was in 1964 that LeWitt exhibited works in his own style incorporating box forms, geometric reliefs and wall structures at the Kaymar Gallery. He went on to develop open cubic forms in modular series. Since 1969 LeWitt has exhibited internationally and participated in shows of Minimal and Conceptual Art. Minimal Art advocated the use of simple hard-edged shapes: the cube, square and grid in configuration or repetition, a limited vocabulary of forms, as a reaction against the personal qualities and gestural brushstrokes of Abstract Expressionism. LeWitt is interested in the artist as thinker and originator of ideas rather than craftsman and has said that 'Conceptual art is made to engage the mind of the viewer rather than his eye or emotions . . . Ideas may be stated with numbers, photographs, or words or any way the artist chooses, the form is unimportant'.[27]

79. Sol Le Witt
Light Cube 1961-62
painted wood, photograph & lightbulb
39 x 30 x 30 cm
Galerie 1900-2000, Marcel Fleiss, Paris and Pierre Huber, Geneva

Untitled (1961-62) fits into LeWitt's early investigations into the nature of ideas and their manifestation in material form. This work is an experiment with the cube form, much as *Box With Random Holes Containing An Object* (1964) and *The Buried Cube* (1968), where a cube, containing an object of importance but little value, is buried. It would appear that these early works deal with notions of interior and exterior space, what is hidden and the simplicity of the structure that is revealed.

George Maciunas 1931-1978

George Maciunas was the founder of Fluxus. He was also the publisher and editor-in-chief, designer and distributor of Fluxus products. Without Maciunas, Fluxus would not have existed.

Maciunas emigrated to America from Lithuania in 1948. He studied art, architecture and graphics at The Cooper Union in New York City until 1952. He went on to receive a degree in architecture and from 1955-60 was involved in postgraduate studies at The Institute of Fine Arts, New York University. It was at this time that he read widely and developed his love of Renaissance music and old musical instruments. He was also interested in the avant-garde music of John Cage and attended classes in electronic music run by Richard Maxfield at the New York School for Social Research, where he met a number of artists, later associated with Fluxus, who had studied with Cage. In 1961 he founded AG Gallery in Madison Avenue where Fluxus was first mentioned. A freelance design job took him to Wiesbaden with the U.S. Army in November 1961. It was during his two years in Germany that he organised the first public Fluxus manifestation, after which he planned a series of Fluxus concerts – 'music actions'. The Fluxus Manifesto was thrown to an audience at Festum Fluxorum in the Art Academy, Düsseldorf in February 1963. It read:

80. George Maciunas
New Flux Year c.1967
box containing pop-out snake
12 x 17 x 7 cm
The Gilbert and Lila Silverman
Fluxus Collection, Detroit

'Purge the world of bourgeois sickness, "intellectual", professional and commercialized culture, PURGE the world of dead art, imitation, artificial art, abstract art, illusionistic art, mathematical art . . . PROMOTE A REVOLUTIONARY FLOOD AND TIDE IN ART, promote living art, anti-art, promote NON ART REALITY to be grasped by all peoples, not only critics, dilettantes and professionals . . .'[28]

Fluxus is a concrete art - what you see is exactly what you get. His *Smile Machine* is precisely that: a device you put in your mouth which forces a smile.

Maciunas' approach was to be simple and direct: to make art cheap, and in a mass-produced form, available in handy, plastic containers, distributed through a centralised network of outlets which circumvented the normal channels of art market exchange. The format plastic boxes Maciunas bought near his home in Canal

Street (the place for buying cheap, surplus manufacturing goods in New York City) were the perfect vehicle for disseminating combinations of Fluxus ideas in a non-hierarchical form.

Maciunas produced most of the graphics for the labels on Fluxus boxes and kits by other artists. He also produced many works himself; some were highly polemical in nature. The Fluxus movement effectively ceased when Maciunas died of cancer in May 1978.

(see also *Fluxus Collective* p.30)

83. Will Maclean
China Nights 1983
painted wood & mirrors
102 x 71.4 x 16 cm
Glasgow Art Gallery and Museum

Will Maclean b.1941

Maclean joined the merchant navy before studying art at Gray's School, Aberdeen between 1961-65. He has been making boxed assemblages since 1974; they are often autobiographical, evoking childhood memories or the history and culture of the Scottish Highlands where Maclean was raised. They also contain references to the role of the sea in the lives of these rural communities, both as a benign and destructive force.

His assemblages are collections of memorabilia and artefacts which suggest many narratives and, at the same time, hidden meanings. Constant in his work is the idea that the mundane elements used – bones, wood, etc. – can be transformed into totems, reliquaries and icons.

China Nights, made from a broken bamboo screen, the wood from the wheelhouse of a boat, mirror and a model boat, is symbolic of voyaging, faraway places – a sailor's dream perhaps.

Man Ray 1890-1976

86. Man Ray
Lips of Gold (Lèvres d'Or)
1967
mixed media
5.2 x 26 x 38.4 cm
Zabriskie Gallery, New York
© Man Ray Trust/DACS, London 1994
(above, closed; below open)

Man Ray was a pioneer of Dada and Surrealism, supporting himself financially as a photographer from 1921 while simultaneously working as a painter, film-maker, writer and maker of objects. He was welcomed into the Parisian avant-garde when he moved to the city from New York in 1921. He stayed in Paris until 1940, but eventually returned in 1951 and lived there until the last years of his life.

Man Ray referred to the many assemblages he made throughout his career as 'Objects of My Affection'. This aptly sums up the visual puns and verbal word-plays they incorporated. By liberating objects from their familiar roles and titling them to highlight their changed identity, the objects were effectively re-born.

Lèvres d'Or (Gold Lips) is a pun on *livre d'or* (meaning both a pound of gold or a gold book for signature by famous visiting house guests). *Gold Lips* is an old book which a bookbinder has transformed into a vanity case by taking out its pages. It both looks and feels like a book but inside is a mirror where your lips, or those of one of Man Ray's models would be reflected. As a motif, lips have appeared in other Man Ray works, most notably in one of his most famous paintings, *Observatory Time – The Lovers* (1934), in which the lips were said to represent 'two bodies fitting together in perfect harmony'.

The starting point for the assemblage *Mr. Knife and Miss Fork* was a drawing Man Ray made in 1931 for a book, *Mr. Knife Miss Fork* by René Crevel. The drawing was never used, but the idea re-surfaced when Man Ray was living in Hollywood in 1944. An assemblage of cord netting holding wooden beads with the knife (representing the masculine) on one side juxtaposed by the fork (representing the feminine) on the other, is bounded by what is really a shallow relief.

Pechage (p.33) is another word-play on both *péche-âge* (peach age) and *péché-age* (age of sin). It has been suggested that the relatively over-sized peaches in comparison with the whole are either 'mythical fruit or Forbidden Fruits of earthly desires'.[29] *Pechage* was editioned in 1964 and *Mr. Knife and Miss Fork* in the 1970s. The resurgence of interest in the work of Man Ray during this period justified the making of other editions: these included *Pandora's Box* in 1960 and *Letter Box* in 1965.

84. Man Ray
Mr Knife and Miss Fork 1944
assemblage of wood, metal, string & tissue
33.8 x 22.8 x 3.7 cm
Lucien Treillard Collection
© Man Ray Trust/DACS, London 1994

Marcel Mariën 1920-1993

In 1937 Mariën met E.L.T. Mesens, Scutenaire, Paul Nougé and Magritte when he first participated in a Surrealist group exhibition. He wrote the first monograph on Magritte in 1943 and collaborated closely with the artist on various publications, which made clear the independence of Belgian Surrealism and attacked the views of French Surrealists, particularly those of André Breton. He edited *View*, an art magazine devoted to Belgian Surrealism (1946) and founded a review, *Naked Lips* (1954). He established the *Prize for Human Stupidity* in 1955, awarding its first and only prize jointly to André Malraux for his work on aesthetics and to the King of Belgium for travelling to the Belgian Congo which became independent after his visit. Since 1967 he has exhibited works in a range of media: collage, drawing, painting, sculpture and assemblage.

The School of Voyeurs is a black, painted box enclosed on three sides, the fourth side is glass through which you can see four rows of desks with open notebooks on the top. On a blackboard at the front of this miniature class room is a picture of a reclining nude. The nude is meant to be viewed through the peephole, as if you were one of the class, looking at this representation of woman as muse. The title Mariën has given to the work suggests something less high-minded – that women after all are just objects for the male gaze.

90. Marcel Mariën
The School of Voyeurs 1971
(detail)
glass fronted box incorporating
small objects
26.8 x 65.1 x 24. 5 cm
Private collection, London
© DACS 1994

108. Patrick Raynaud
*Fantin-Latour's Suitcase:
Homage to Delacroix 1989*
illuminated cibachrome
photographs & flight cases
170 x 62 x 60 cm each (closed)
The artist
© ADAGP, Paris & DACS, London 1994

75. Jiří Kolář
Nest Box 1974
chiasmage on wooden nest box
108.6 x 72.5 x 75 cm
Musée National d'Art Moderne,
Centre Georges Pompidou, Paris
© DACS 1994

104. Mimi Parent
Eve Rêve 1973
mixed media
92.7 x 62.2 x 14 cm
Danielle Boile Collection, France

76. Françoise Lacampagne
*Energie Dissipative (Homage
to Yves Klein) 1990*
wood, stone & pigment
each part 63 x 38 x 21 cm
J.P. Ledeur, Paris
© ADAGP, Paris & DACS, London 1994

121. Kurt Schwitters
'3' 1922
inlaid wooden box
6.8 x 16.7 x 9.4 cm
Marlborough International Fine Art
© DACS 1994

40. William Christenberry
Klan Dolls 1992
mixed media
10.1 x 67.3 x 47 cm
The artist

117. Lucas Samaras
Box No. 32 1965
Wood, artificial hair & bones
33 x 25.4 x 38.1 cm
Saatchi Collection, London

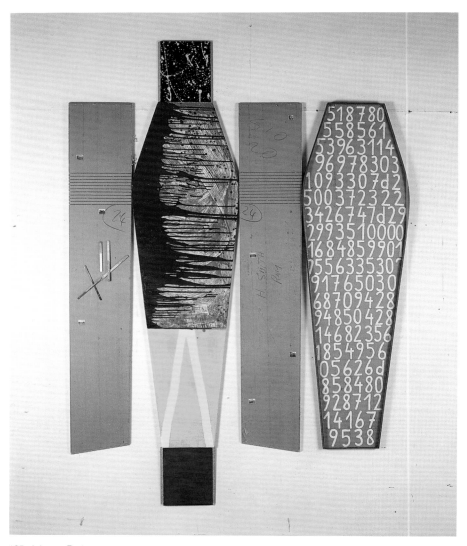

135. Johanes Zechner
A Boy 1993
acrylic, household paint &
collage on chipboard coffin
251 x 178 x 6 cm
Francis Graham-Dixon Gallery,
London

91. Larry Miller
Sunflower 1985
satin-lined box containing
dead sunflower
55 x 39 cm
Henry Buhl, New York

Robert Morris b.1931

Robert Morris studied engineering and art in Kansas City. He
continued his studies at the California School for Fine Arts,
returning to San Francisco (after army service) and worked in
improvisatory theatre, film and painting. In 1961 he moved to New
York where he made his first sculptures, writing a dissertation on
Brancusi for his art history course at Humber College between
1962-63. He was briefly associated with the Pop Art movement,
but then cited as a Minimalist with Carl André, Dan Flavin and
Donald Judd among others: however, to describe Morris as a
Minimalist does not do justice to his inventiveness as a sculptor.

Untitled 1963 also exists in bronze. Here the box is an irreconcilable
contradiction, its function denied by the instructions on the door. By
refusing to be a functional object, it is elevated to the status of art.

Untitled 1963 was one of a series of early boxes Morris made that
carry information: *Box with Sound of Its Own Making* (a cube
containing a tape recorder, which plays over three hours, the noises
created whilst making the box); the *I Box* (in which an I-shaped
door opens to show a full-length nude photograph of the artist).

92. Robert Morris
Untitled 1963
paint on wood, metal & padlock
28 x 20 x 9 cm
Sonnabend Collection

93. Charles Murray
Snuff Box 1950
mahogany, oil, pen & ink,
brass nails, inlay & cork
5 x 3.8 x 10.7 cm
Andrew Murray

Charles Murray 1894 - 1954

Between 1919 and 1925 Charles Murray studied at Glasgow School
of Art and the British School in Rome, after which he served in the
Russian White Army. In 1926 he joined the staff at Glasgow School
of Art achieving a reputation as a printmaker. He left abruptly in
1932 and settled in Yorkshire. He painted in oil, mostly landscapes
conjured from memory by notes and models of subjects he wanted
to represent. Murray demonstrated considerable manual skill,
evident in this small painted snuff box, part of a series of similar
objects he made shortly before his death.[30]

Louise Nevelson 1899 - 1988

In 1905 Nevelson emigrated from Russia with her family to join her
father in Maine, where he was a builder and owner of lumber
yards. In 1920 she married Charles Nevelson and moved to New
York City. In 1929 - 30 she studied at the Art Student League and in
1935 took part in her first group exhibition at the Brooklyn
Museum. At that time she made small figurative sculptures of
polychromed plaster, terracotta and bronze.

Nevelson did not achieve real recognition until 1958 with her
exhibition of sculptural walls at Grand Central Moderns Gallery. By
this time she had been working over 30 years, experimenting with
a wide variety of media. She had made important visits to Mexico,
to the Mayan ruins (1950), and travelled in Central America to the
Yucatan Peninsula and Guatemala (1951): the stelae, altars and
architectural sculptures she saw there had a lasting impact on
her art.

It has been said that Nevelson made sculpture in a wooden box
after receiving some bottles of alcohol in a crate, or that she found
a box in the street and took it home. Nevelson said after the

Second World War, 'I began to see things, almost anything along the street as art . . . that's why I pick up old wood that had a life, that cars have gone over . . . All my objects are retranslated. That's the magic.'[31]

It was probable that Nevelson found box-forms a suitable framing device for the relief constructions she made inside them. She certainly used to stack her box sculptures against the studio walls, which may have been the precedent for her wall environments like *Moon Garden + One* (1958).

Nevelson only used white, gold and black to colour these works – black was the principal colour. At first the walls were constructed in shallower reliefs (late 1950s) but by the late 1960s the recesses could be deep enough to contain another box form. *Night-Focus-Dawn* has been called 'the zenith of her wood sculpture . . . Box within a box, an irregular; linear, expressive, fragile fruit crate played in contrapuntal composition of enormous subtlety against a manufactured box'.[32] In front of these closed fruit crates are elongated points which overlap the box form, the triangular element with its curved side giving a flowing rhythm to the whole. There are subtle changes where sometimes boxes are placed up-side-down, their punctured surfaces creating other visual rhythms. Nevelson said, 'I use action and counteraction, like in music all the time.'[33]

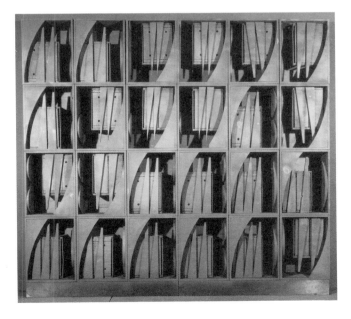

95. Louise Nevelson
Night-Focus-Dawn 1969
24 painted wood boxes on base
259.1 x 297.2 x 35.6 cm
Whitney Museum of American Art:
Purchased with funds from
Howard and Jean Lipman

Avis Newman b.1946

Since the early 1980s the motif of the bird has been both a metaphor for flight and a symbol of intellectual and creative freedom in Newman's painting and sculpture. *Bird Box Scatola dell'Uccello* and *Object From Nature* relate to a series of boxes dating from 1984 that have incorporated drawn representations, bird fragments or implied a bird's presence through titling. *Bird Box Scatola dell'Uccello* 'in particular indicates the voyeuristic aspect of viewing, where the representations are both double-sided and absent'.[34]

For Newman the box form can perfectly contain the duality of things as both objects and representations and their correspondence to language.

97. Avis Newman
Cyphers Which Supply A Place But Signify Nothing 1990
box with wax, snail shells & plastic
23 x 9.8 x 5.3 cm
Lisson Gallery, London

Claes Oldenburg b.1929

Oldenburg was born in Sweden but settled in Chicago in 1936. He studied art and literature at Yale University between 1946-1950. He moved to New York in 1956 where he took part in 'Happenings' and was involved with Fluxus during the early 1960s while emerging as the major sculptor of American Pop Art.

In 1966 Oldenburg wished to extend his *Colossal Monuments* project to London and Stockholm. His idea was to enlarge everyday objects and insert them into appropriate sites in a given cityscape. The inspiration for *London Knees* came from the miniskirt; Oldenburg made a visit to London in July 1966 and was very aware of a liberation of knees on the city streets. He also felt that the formal qualities of the knee were mirrored in some of the architecture of the city. Oldenburg eventually found his ideal knees in a warehouse of discarded mannequins; only one knee suited his purpose so he corrected the deficiencies of the other by recasting it. Inside the case the knees are wrapped in felt socks, but can stand on their plexiglass platform as a model for a proposed monument. The lithographs show the knees as monumental columns, as a bridge over the Thames, a gigantic sculpture on Embankment . . . Other documents inside the case draw attention to the many processes necessary to fully realise an artistic idea.

Double Nose/Purse/Punching Bag/Ashtray is a personal diary in object form, but one that deliberately evades and conceals its meaning . A facsimile notebook with sketches and writings about the development of the box was excluded from the final version by the artist since he felt it would destroy its mystery.[35] It is also an evocation of the landscape of Northern California as shown by the redwood box and bark chips.

99. Claes Oldenburg
London Knees 1966-68
cast latex painted with
coloured polyurethane, felt,
cast acrylic, 21 offset
lithographs on paper in cloth
covered travelling case
27 x 41 x 39 cm
Arts Council Collection, South Bank
Centre, London

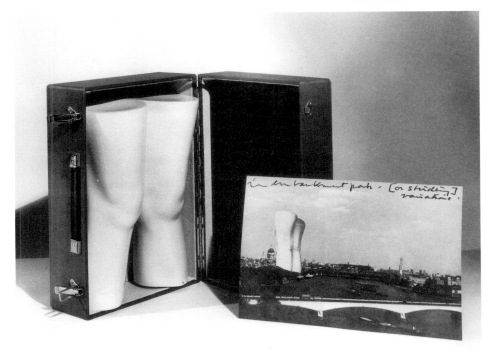

Yoko Ono b.1933

The Ono family moved from Japan to New York City in 1952, where Ono studied music at Sarah Lawrence College. Through her first marriage to pianist Tochi Ichiyonagi she came into contact with John Cage and Merce Cunningham. Her loft in Chambers Street was famous in serious art circles for its concerts. It was

101. Yoko Ono
All White Chess Set 1962-70
acrylic on wood
3.4 x 17.1 x 12.7 cm
Arts Council Collection, South Bank Centre, London

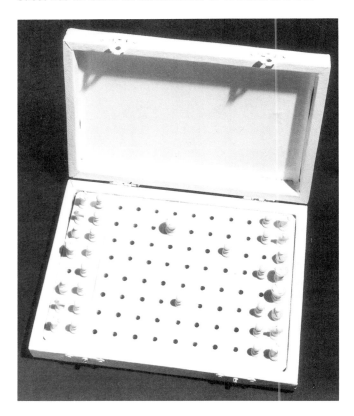

Cage's theories of chance and audience involvement that influenced Ono's own early performances, such as *Bicycle Piece for Orchestra* (1962) where 100 cyclists pedalled noiselessly around the stage. She came to London in the late 1960s: her film *Bottoms*, a montage of 365 backsides causing a scandal. It was her association with and subsequent marriage to John Lennon in 1968 that gave her celebrity status but this relationship overshadowed her seriousness as an artist. Yoko Ono made objects between 1960-71: *All White Chess Set* is a pocket variation of a Fluxus work. Ono regarded chess as combative – a war game on a board. As a fervent pacifist, she defeats potential adversaries by painting both areas of the board white – white also being the colour of surrender.

Meret Oppenheim 1913-1985

Meret Oppenheim is best known for *Le Déjeuner en Fourrure*, a cup, saucer and spoon covered with the fur of a Chinese gazelle; for many this epitomises the ultimate Surrealist art work, but its 'fame' has certainly overshadowed her considerable artistic output of drawings, paintings, collages, assemblages and sculpture.

Oppenheim's move to Paris in 1932 led her to mix in Surrealist circles until 1937, which had a beneficial effect on her art. She moved to Switzerland permanently in 1939 and intermittently suffered a depressive crisis which lasted until 1954. She made *Box with Wood Grate* in 1943 , an animal hutch containing a mirror, pebbles, balls and butterfly wings. The effect is of a cage, not surprisingly, given Oppenheim's state of mind and the fact that it was war-time. It was not until the 1960s and early 1970s that she began to make objects/assemblages again (she had produced significant assemblages in the 1930s), such as *The Cocoon (It's Alive)* of 1974. When the cushion is moved back and forth in your hand, the mercury shifts.

103. Meret Oppenheim
The Cocoon (Its Alive) 1974
box of wood with cover of plexiglass, cushion of satin with filling of mercury & branches
9 x 16 x 13 cm
Birgit and Burkhard Wenger, Basel
© DACS 1994

Mimi Parent b.1924

Mimi Parent studied at the École des Beaux-Arts in Montreal, before moving to Paris with her husband Jean Benoit in 1948. In 1959 she met André Breton and participated in Surrealist exhibitions throughout the 1960s and 1970s. Her works are often constructed in the manner of a stage set, on which is enacted a dream-tableau (p.59).

Attributed to **Roland Penrose** 1900-1984

Roland Penrose was at the forefront of the British Surrealist movement, both as an artist and writer. He organised the first International Surrealist Exhibition in 1936 (see Agar p. 8) and ran the London Gallery between 1937-39. After the war in 1947 he co-founded the Institute of Contemporary Arts, London, first serving as its Chairman and then as President from 1969-76.

105. Attributed to
Roland Penrose
Untitled 1946-50
oil paint inside perspex box
8.2 x 12.7 x 1.7 cm
Private collection, on loan to the
Penrose Collection, England

No documentation exists conclusively proving that this painted cigarette box is by Penrose, but the painted motifs and use of colour do bear a close correspondence to his work of the period.

Robert Rauschenberg b.1925

Rauschenberg moved to New York in 1949 after studying art at the Kansas City Art Institute and attending the Académie Julian in Paris. In 1952 Rauschenberg travelled to Europe and North Africa with Cy Twombly (whom he had met with John Cage and Merce Cunningham in 1949 while attending Black Mountain College). This extended journey was well-documented by Rauschenberg – the objects and environments he photographed surfaced in later works. He also produced three distinct bodies of work: small-scale collages, hanging and boxed assemblages. He found his materials in flea-markets and old bookstalls, but the boxed works also contain organic materials – skulls, insects, beetles, twigs, snail shells and bones. Their minute scale was necessarily determined by Rauschenberg's travelling from place to place. Their simplicity and concentration on one or two elements suggest a kind of reliquary or votive offering.

On his return from Europe, Rauschenberg created 19 *Elemental Sculptures*, assembled from rubbish near his Fulton Street studio.

These were three-dimensional works made from simple materials – wood blocks joined by twine to stones or packing crates with spikes, nails and stones – for an exhibition at the Stable Gallery in the autumn of 1953. Only nine works still survive. *Music Box* was intended to be handled so that the stones would strike the nails making a percussive music of clanks and clonks. At the same time Joseph Cornell (p. 22) was also making music boxes, but these were sealed, the 'music' made by the jangling of trinkets inside.

107. Robert Rauschenberg
Music Box (Elemental Sculpture) 1953
wood, nails, 3 pebbles & feather
30 x 19.6 x 23.5 cm
Jasper Johns Collection
© The artist/DACS, London/VAGA, New York 1994

Patrick Raynaud b.1946

Since the mid-1980s much of Raynaud's work has been concerned with the present-day position of artists on the international art circuit, whom Raynaud has likened to the great painter-decorators of the past, who practised their trade by travelling around the great courts of Europe. Raynaud has conceived works – for example, *The Tower of Princess X . . .* or *The Art of Travel* and *Transports* (1987); *Roller Box-Sculpture in Transit* (1988) and *Art Flight Cases* (1989) and here Cousin's and Fantin-Latour's suitcases (p.57) – which have their basis in the physical, monetary and cultural exchanges that take place within the art world.

For Raynaud, the secondary material of exhibition-making has become the primary material of his art: the packing crate and the photograph of the art work. Raynaud's point is both ironic and economic when you consider what a high percentage of an exhibition budget is paid to packers/art shippers and in making reproductions of art works. In his series of artists' suitcases Raynaud 're-invents' 19th century French masterpieces by Courbet, as well as Fantin-Latour and Cousin. The photographic reproductions of particular paintings seen here once more become original works of art. Raynaud highlights the interventionist and subversive role a contemporary artist can play in an art world where the original, rare work of art is often a bartering chip among the power-brokers who manage the major museum collections. This particular series also makes us look anew at how we view works of art – the reproduction is usually how we *recognise* a work of art without *experiencing* its presence.

109. Patrick Raynaud
Cousin's suitcase, Eva Prima Pandora 1990
illuminated cibachrome photograph & flight case
70 x 150 x 50 cm (closed)
The artist
© ADAGP, Paris & DACS, London 1994

Martial Raysse b.1936

In his artist's statement, 'I have a thousand things to put in order . . .', which was glued into the back of his exhibition catalogue published by the Dwan Gallery in 1967, Raysse said, 'I wanted my works to

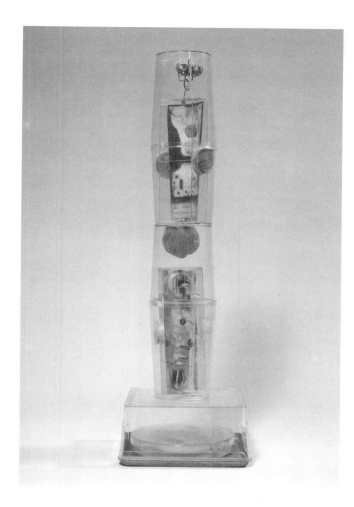

110. Martial Raysse
Nécropolis II 1960
objects in perspex boxes
68 x 20 x 20 cm
Private collection, Sweden;
Courtesy of Galerie Bonnier,
Geneva
© ADAGP, Paris & DACS, London 1994

possess the serene self-evidence of mass-produced refrigerators
. . . to have the look of new sterile unalterable visual hygiene . . . I
wish to emphasise that my works do not employ variable elements
but variable geometry.'

Raysse, one of the founder members of the *Nouveaux Réalistes*
(see Arman p. 8 and César p. 19), first started to encapsulate
diverse objects in perspex boxes in 1958. By 1960 he produced
more ambitious column structures of interconnecting perspex
boxes containing objects as diverse as plastic knives, forks, shaving
brushes, syringes, garlic crushers, toothpicks, sunglasses and
flowers. These cheap, garish, manufactured objects emphasised
the meaningless wealth of choice in consumer society. In
Nécropolis the objects combine to form a strange hybrid creature, a
monstrous creation of the consumer age.

Florence Régnier-Barral b.1946

Florence Régnier-Barral makes architectural box reliefs using plaster and mosaic. The crevices and indentations of these solitary spaces are animated by sand and the action of light and shadow. Her series *Inside Out* goes further, creating illusionistic depth and height by a judicious use of mirrors extending the architecture of the box to infinity.

111. Florence Régnier-Barral
Untitled 1989
(from the series *Places*)
plaster, wood, mosaic & sand
40 x 99.5 x 13 cm
The artist

James Riddle b.1933

There were many Fluxus packagings of *ESP Flux Kit*. The work was issued as an individual edition and as a component in some *Flux Kits*.[36]

113. James Riddle
Flux Clock Cabinet 1966
25 clockfaces, 1 clock, 1 cabinet
circa 38 x 38 x 38 cm
The Gilbert and Lila Silverman
Fluxus Collection, Detroit

Larry Rivers b.1923

Larry Rivers began his career as a jazz saxophonist, studying composition at the Juilliard School of Music and playing in jazz bands in and around New York between 1940-45. He started painting in 1945 and later attended Hans Hofmann's School of Painting. Rivers is perhaps best known for his modification of Pop Art iconography – advertising, bank notes, cigarette packets – the important difference being that Rivers did not create facsimiles (Andy Warhol's Campbell Soup cans or Brillo boxes) but re-created the original in the free style of an Abstract Expressionist. In the 1960s Rivers experimented with extending the picture plane by fixing materials such as wood, metal, plastic and plaster to its surface.

115. Larry Rivers
Webster and Cigars 1962
mixed media & collage on wood
32.7 x 40.6 x 40 cm
The artist
© The artist/DACS, London/VAGA,
New York 1994

In 1961 Rivers made a series of paintings based on Daniel Webster's picture originally found on a cigar box. Daniel Webster was a hero (in common with Rivers' other favoured subjects, Napoleon and George Washington). He has repeatedly returned to the Webster motif in paintings dated between 1963-64 and again in 1979. *Webster and Cigars* is the only known boxed assemblage of the subject.

Takako Saito b.1929

In the 1960s Saito left Japan for New York City, where she lived until 1968. She collaborated with George Maciunas (p. 59) in the fabrication of *Fluxgames*. She lived in France from 1968-72 where she made contact with George Brecht (p.16) and Robert Filliou (p. 29). Since 1979 Saito has lived in Düsseldorf.

Saito organised meetings, performances and games where she transformed chess by replacing the traditional pieces with glasses of wine, fake jewels, nuts and bolts, sandwiches, vials of perfume (smell chess), spices or, as seen here, grinders, borers and piercers. By determining the denomination of the pieces by smell, weight, colour and texture, Saito added a whole new dimension and complication to the game.

116. Takako Saito
Flux Chess: Grinder Chess
c. 1965-70
wooden box containing 28 chess pieces (blue & white buffer brushes & grinding stones)
17 x 17 x 7.4 cm
Tate Gallery Archives

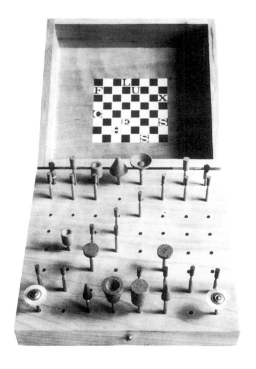

Lucas Samaras b.1936

Lucas Samaras is a painter, photographer and film-maker, and studied at Rutgers University between 1955-59, followed by studies in art history at Columbia University in 1959 with Allan Kaprow and George Segal. Lucas Samaras made his first boxes in 1960: 'I was using things that were partly ruined or about to be

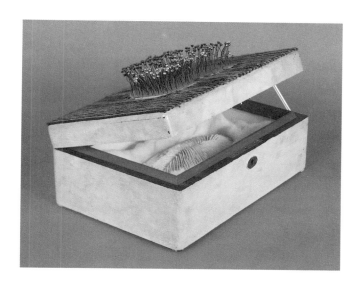

120. Lucas Samaras
Untitled late 1960s
Box containing sea coral,
cotton wool wth pins & yarns
16.5 x 30.5 x 21 cm
The Mayor Gallery

thrown away. I think I was interested in the idea that when
something became useless I could rescue it and give it a dignity it
never had.'[37]

These first experiments were generally monochromatic and crude –
containing plastered rags and crêpe paper – compared with the
ornate, baroque quality of some of his later work. Samaras usually
bought or found Victorian boxes to work with, particularly those
with drop shelving, drawers and compartments that could hold
secrets. He covered all their surfaces with objects or textures,
seemingly obsessed by the patterns, colour and overall richness of
effect, and sometimes contradictory juxtapositions: for example,
sharp pins with soft cotton. From 1962 he started to cover boxes
with pins, fascinated by how light caught and reflected on the
metallic surface; the following year he introduced wool knitting
yarns as a motif. His repertory of motifs built continuously
throughout the 1960s to include jewels, food, photographs and cut-
out paper drawings.

Samaras made three room structures in the 1960s. The first was
his room recreated as a work of art (1964). The room acted as a
container of personal history, a self-portrait, making the spectator a
voyeur into the artist's life. *The Mirrored Room* (1966) was covered
with mirrored panels inside and out, a narcissistic container
reflecting an image of self to infinity. The room on show at the
Whitechapel Art Gallery was designed in 1967 and first shown at
Documenta in 1968. Again, it is mirrored inside and out, but it is
also a reflecting fortress, large mirrored points act as a warning.
The room does not refuse entry, but does not encourage it either.
The low door, only three feet high, makes access difficult. Above
the door, as you stand up, is a large point threatening to hit your
head. This is in fact a torture chamber.

122. Kurt Schwitters
To Roland Peppenrose
5 April 1940
pencil drawing on opened-out
cigarette box
7.3 x 14.6 cm
Private collection: Courtesy of
The Mayor Gallery
© DACS 1994

Kurt Schwitters 1887-1948

'. . . all values exist only in so far as they are related to one another
and that to confine oneself to one material is one-sided and limited.
That is how I came to form MERZ, the sum total of art in its various
forms – MERZ-painting, MERZ-writing. It is my ultimate
object to combine art and non art in a MERZ-*Gesamtweltbild,* a
world embracing MERZ-picture . . .' (1919)[38]

Schwitters studied art in Dresden and Hanover between 1908 and
1914. Until 1917 he painted academic pictures, but the First World
War changed many of his perceptions. After the war he wrote,
'new things had to be made out of the fragments: and this is Merz
– it is like an image of the revolution within me, not as it was, but
as it should have been.'[39] From this time Schwitters was involved
with the Der Sturm group and thereafter associated with both Dada
and the pioneers of abstract art (Moholy-Nagy, Mondrian and
Lissitzky).

Schwitters broke away from the picture plane by collaging
elements to its surface. From this process evolved his relief
constructions. The logical consequence of all these explorations
was his *Merzbau,* built in Hanover. He used all the walls of the
room as a picture surface, building a structure that redefined the
architecture of the space, surrounding the spectator.

On p. 61 is one example of a series of boxes that Schwitters made
in the early 1920s. It is consistent with Schwitters writings,
showing that any material or structure could be combined in
making his art. During this period Schwitters also made several
boxes based on his famous collection of poems, *Anna Blume.*

Schwitters left Nazi Germany in 1933, spending seven years in
Norway. He came to England in 1940. He tried to begin creating a
new *Merzbau* in a barn in Westmorland: what remains can be seen
at the Hatton Gallery, University of Newcastle.

Daniel Spoerri b.1930

Daniel Spoerri was born in Romania, but his family fled the Holocaust and settled in Switzerland in 1941. He had many changes of occupation in his early life working variously as an apprentice bookseller, a fruitseller, labourer and waiter. By 1954 he had become the principal dancer at the Bern Opera, after studying classical dance in Paris two years previously. He staged several avant-garde plays including collaborating with Meret Oppenheim (p.71) and taught mime and jazz choreography. In 1957-59 he set up *Edition MAT* and published art works in multiple editions by Arman (a homage to Arman's accumulations appears in this exhibition), Duchamp and Man Ray. Spoerri has said that the making of an art work is analogous to cooking a meal. He was involved with now legendary food projects – artists' dinner 'events' held at various galleries throughout the 1960s. He opened the Restaurant Spoerri (1968) and the Eat Art Gallery (1970) in Düsseldorf; his continuing preoccupation with food led him to write *Mythology and Meatballs. A Greek Island Diary/Cookbook* in 1982. Spoerri first made works in boxes and drawers in 1961 and has subsequently used containers in a series of assemblages made in 1984.

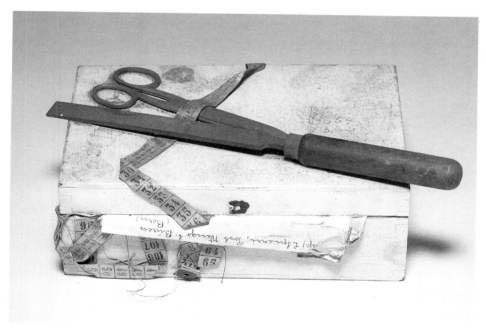

123. Daniel Spoerri
Vera's Sewing Kit 1960
mixed media
8 x 23 x 15 cm
Sonnabend Collection
© ADAGP, Paris & DACS, London 1994

Fred Stiven b.1929

Fred Stiven started to make box constructions in the late 1960s. All the elements are made from wood, which have been bent, honed, turned, or cut into the specific shapes Stiven requires. These are arranged within a case he constructs, but are not permanently fixed until he has lived with a chosen composition for a suitable length of time. The different wooden pieces are then painted; Stiven's colour range is muted – white, cream, grey, grey-green, slate-blue – but has the effect of coordinating the rhythm of his arrangements.

Between 1946-51 Fred Stiven studied at Edinburgh College of Art. He taught at Gray's School of Art, Aberdeen from 1959, retiring as Head of Design in 1987.

125. Fred Stiven
Dark Box 1975
mixed media
27 x 15 x 10 cm
The artist

Ben Vautier b.1935

Ben (more usually known by his first name) was self-taught as an artist. In 1958 he bought a shop where he sold second-hand records and showed exhibitions including works by Martial Raysse (p.74) in 1959. He named his gallery *Ben Doute de Tout* (Ben

128. Ben Vautier
Flux Box Containing God c.1966
plastic box
9.3 x 12 x 16 cm
The Gilbert and Lila Silverman
Fluxus Collection, Detroit
© ADAGP, Paris & DACS, London 1994

doubts everything). At this time he started to make paintings – usually white handwritten letters on a black background, with words or banal sentences. In 1962 he became closely involved with Fluxus and participated in many performances throughout the 1960s; he was certainly one of the most radical artists associated with the movement. He also made containers, the most outrageous being his *Fluxbox Containing God*. For Ben, everything was art, even himself, he even developed the slogan *Art = Ben*. Ben also argued that if God were everywhere, he could make Him present by signing objects with His name '*Dieu*'.

131. Paule Vézelay
Lines in Space No 56 1969
painted wood & string
50 x 54.5 x 11 cm
Estate of Paule Vézelay, England
& Co. Gallery, London

Paule Vézelay 1892-1984

Paule Vézelay was born Marjorie Watson-Williams. She studied painting and etching at Bristol Municipal School of Art before moving to London in 1912. She was a member of the London Group from 1922-33. In 1926 she settled in Paris and changed her name in homage to the church at Vézelay and to symbolise her affinity with the artists making up the School of Paris. In 1928 she produced her first purely abstract work.

In 1935 she began her *Recherches en Trois Dimensions – tableaux de Fil et Ficelles Tendus*. 'I first made small wooden cases into which I stretched fishing lines, cotton threads and fine cords; these formed straight lines and contrasting angles in space. For curves I used dried leaves and cut out flat forms, collage in fact . . . I was soon using various kinds of wire which gave me three-dimensional lines which could be curved or undulated (sic) in any direction I desired . . . My lines in space create a third element by casting their shadows, and these changing delicate echoes seemed to add depth and light and beauty to the whole construction; they had, as all shadows have for me, a quality of magic. It is now almost 30 years since I began to make these simple experiments. Modest as they were they became more varied as the years went on; they have already been widely exploited by others'. [40]

Vézelay exhibited her *Lines in Space* at the Galerie Jeanne Bucher, Paris in 1937. She returned to England in 1939 at the outbreak of war, and continued to experiment with forms of abstraction, exhibiting widely until her death.

Robert Watts 1923-1987

133. Robert Watts
Flux Atlas 1973
plastic box containing stones
& printed cards
212 x 32.7 x 5.7 cm
The Gilbert and Lila Silverman
Fluxus Collection, Detroit

Robert Watts studied engineering at the University of Louisville between 1942-44. He attended the Art Student League from 1946-48. He also studied art history at Columbia University and received his Masters in 1951. From 1946-58 he essentially followed the tradition of Abstract Expressionism. In 1958 he stopped painting,

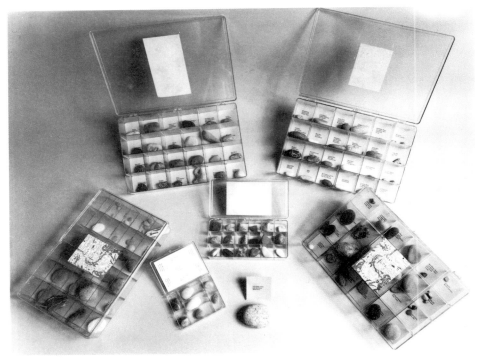

instead producing a number of electrical and kinetic works. Watts was involved in Fluxus from 1962. From 1970 he became increasingly interested in archaeology, science and nature. Several works of this period incorporate parts of dead animals; for example, *Flux Archaeology with Flat Mouse* and *Art Rat Box.*

134. Huang Yongping
The history of Chinese art and the history of modern Western art washed in a washing machine for two minutes 1987
(this version re-made 1993)
mixed media
80 x 50 x 50 cm
The artist

Huang Yongping b.1954

Huang Yongping studied at the Zheijiang Academy of Fine Arts in Hangzhou until 1982. He then worked for seven years as a secondary school teacher, after which he left China for France. In 1986 he became a founder and main participant in the Xiamen Dada group which made performances and Happenings, very much in the iconoclastic spirit of their 1920s European counterparts. Yongping uses washing machines in his work as a symbol of cleansing and purification. Here two art historical texts are pulped. As Yongping has said, ' Because history cannot speak for itself, the only things left are words and writing. We are in the middle of a huge rubbish heap. If we do not leave this rubbish heap we will continue to be oppressed by all kinds of ideologies, values and ideas on morality.'41

Johanes Zechner b.1953

The box has been a prevalent form in Johanes Zechner's work since he came to London between 1987-88 on a British Council Fellowship to study at the Royal College of Art. Zechner does not buy a box for its contents, is not seduced by its packaging – he takes what has been discarded and uses the inside, the once outside faces the wall. This recycling gives renewed life to the object as a 'sculpture drawing'. Zechner's use of colour and collage is determined by the creases, tucks and folds that were part of the box's previous three-dimensional existence unlike Schwitters (p.80) and Picasso who opened out used packets, but their drawings took no account of the schematic arrangement of verticals and horizontals.

The coffin pieces (p.64) are an extension of this idea – to both flatten and reveal what has been of no importance, or in this case, perhaps, culturally taboo. *A Boy* was created from a batch of English coffins Zechner bought in South Wimbledon, numbers of measurements scrawled by the maker have become part of the art work. Zechner is interested both by the formal possibilities of these objects and their cultural identity; coffin shapes are not standardised, differing between countries.

136. Johanes Zechner
Gepäck! The Big Issue 1993
acrylic paint & collage on canvas (17 pieces) for a suitcase
circa 325 x 380 cm
Collection Schömer, Klosterneuburg, Austria

137. Krystyna Ziach
Memory of Rain 1993
wood box, mirror &
photograph
41 x 48 x 6 cm
Private collection

Krystyna Ziach b.1953

Between 1973-1979 Krystyna Ziach studied sculpture and art
history in Poland. In 1979 she moved to Holland and studied
graphics and photography.

The *Memory of Rain* box is a multiple version of a large-scale
sculpture made for an installation entitled *A Garden of Illusion*,
which examined the relationship between sculptural form and
photography and that of illusionistic space created by the use of
mirrors. Here a blue-tinted photograph of houses, inserted into the
cut-out lid, is reflected in a mirror in the base. Effectively, the box is
created by two frames joined together.

Notes

1. Eileen Agar, *A Look at My Life,* Methuen, London, 1988, p.121.

2. H. Martin, *Arman,* Harry N. Abrams, New York, 1973 quoted on inside dustjacket.

3. Letter to the author from Jane Hart, L.A. Louver Gallery, 13 September 1993.

4. Carin Kouni (ed.), *Energy Plan for the Western Man. Joseph Beuys in America. Writings by and Interviews with the Artist,* Four Walls Eight Windows, New York, 1990, p.19.

5. J. Schellmann, *Joseph Beuys: Multiples. Catalogue Raisonné of Multiples and Prints 1965-1985,* Schellmann, Munich, 1985.

6. Gijs van Tuyl, 'Space for Boezem' in *Marinus Boezem,* XX Sao Paulo Bienal 1989

7. Letter to the author, 1 October 1993.

8. Printed in *Boîtes,* Musée d'Art Moderne de la Ville de Paris and Maison de la Culture de Rennes, 1977. Translation by the author.

9. Jon Hendricks (ed.), *Fluxus Codex,* The Gilbert and Lila Silverman Fluxus Collection, Detroit, Michigan in association with Harry N. Abrams, New York, 1988, p.189. Much information on Fluxus works comes from this extensive volume. Future references are prefaced by op. cit. FC and the page number.

10. op. cit. FC p.215.

11. The progression of his work was such that a number of large-scale, back-lit transparencies of the interiors of these peephole boxes were made into a gallery installation *Access* at the Collins Gallery, University of Strathclyde in 1992. The one-time interior became an exterior space contained within the enclosure of the gallery.

12. op. cit. FC p.223.

13. Walter Hopps, 'Klan Dolls' in *Grand Street* No. 44, W.E., Barnett and Associates, Houston, p.95.

14. *Jeffrey Dennis,* Orchard Gallery, 13 February - 13 March 1993, p.28-29.

15. Marcel Duchamp interviewed by James John Sweeney, 1995 reproduced in Arturo Schwarz, *The Complete Works of Marcel Duchamp,* Thames and Hudson, London, 1969, p.513.

16. *A View From Back O'Town, Anthony Earnshaw: Work 1945-1987,* Leeds City Art Gallery, 1987, n.p.

17. André Breton, 'Du surréalisme en ses oeuvres vives' in *Manifesto du Surréalisme,* ed. Idées Gallimard, Paris, p.182.

18. Interview with Robert Filliou 1970, reprinted in Charles Dreyfus, *Happenings and Fluxus,* Galerie 1900-2000, Galerie de Genie and Galerie de Poche, 1989, p.62. Translation by the author.

19. For a fuller account, see *Richard Hamilton*, Tate Gallery, London, 1992, p.172.

20. op. cit. FC p.264.

21. op. cit. FC p.263.

22. Interview with Catherine Lacey in *Susan Hiller, Belshazzar's Feast, The Artist's View*, Tate Gallery, London 1985, p.13.

23. op. cit. FC pp.278-279.

24. op. cit. FC p.294.

25. Eva Neumannová, 'In Quest of Art' in *Jiří Kolář Koláze Objekty*, Národní Galerie, Prague, 1993.

26. Letter to the author, 16 February 1994.

27. Sol LeWitt, 'Paragraphs on Conceptual Art', *Artforum*, New York, vol.5, no.10 (June 1967), pp.79-83.

28. op. cit. FC p.24.

29. A. Schwarz, *Man Ray: The Rigour of Imagination*, Thames and Hudson, London, 1977, p.200.

30. Information on the artist, kindly supplied by Andrew Murray.

31. Jean Lipman, *Nevelson's World*, Hudson Hills Press in association with the Whitney Museum of American Art, New York, 1983.

32. Arnold B. Glimcher, *Louise Nevelson*, Dutton, New York, revised edition 1976, p.163.

33. *Louise Nevelson*, exhibition catalogue, Whitney Museum of American Art, New York, 1987, p.13.

34. Unpublished statement by artist.

35. For further information see *Claes Oldenburg Multiples in Retrospect, 1964-1990*, Rizzoli, New York, pp.58-69 and 98-107.

36. op. cit. FC p.450.

37. Kim Levin, *Lucas Samaras*, Harry N. Abrams Inc., New York, 1975, p.26.

38. Reprinted in *Kurt Schwitters Retrospective*, Marlborough-Gerson Gallery Inc., New York, May-June 1965, p.14.

39. op. cit. FC.

40. Comments on Paule Vézelay's 'Lines in Space' published in *The Tate Gallery Report*, London 1963-64, p.45.

41. *Silent Energy*, MOMA, Oxford, 27 June - 29 August 1993, p.16.

Exhibition checklist

Works in this exhibition are mostly available for loan throughout the hour. The key below indicates which works are unable to travel to all the venues:

Edinburgh only *   London only **   Norwich and London only ***
Sheffield excluded ****   all venues except Edinburgh *****

1. Eileen Agar**
Untitled 1936
watercolour, corals, sea horse, eye of Horus amulet, feather & lace in a wooden box
15.8 x 22.6 x 5.3 cm
Oliver Murray

2. Arman
Full Up 1960
sardine tin (with dust & key enclosed)
10.5 x 6 x 3 cm
Paul Martin

3. Arman
The Village of the Damned 1962
dolls in display vitrine
53 x 51 x 28 cm
Dagny Runnqvist Collection, Geneva

4. Ay-O
Tactile Box 1963
cardboard box stamped with hole in top
31 x 31 x 31.5 cm
The Gilbert and Lila Silverman Fluxus Collection, Detroit

5. Ay-O
Finger Box 1964/65
cardboard box stamped with hole in top
8.5 x 9.5 x 9.5 cm
Galerie 1900-2000, Marcel Fleiss, Paris

6. Clive Barker
Zip Box No. 1 1963
leather & metal zip
31 x 13 x 15.5 cm
Tieuli Collection, Venice

7. Clive Barker
Cremated Richard Hamilton Painting 1971
wood casket & ashes
17.5 x 25.2 x 21.7 cm
The artist

8. Mary Bauermeister
Needless Needles 1964
wood, glass, ink, watercolour & objects
96 x 63 x 15 cm
Rolf and Doris Renker, Düren

9. Mary Bauermeister
Homage to Quentin Metsys 1969
wood & glass
53 x 53 x 17 cm
Diter and Sigrid Löw

10. Mary Bauermeister
Pyramid 1977
glass, ink, wood & sand
60 x 60 x 60 cm
Doris Stockhausen, Cologne

11. Tony Berlant
Luchita No.68 1990
found metal collage on plywood with steel brads
64.7 x 53.4 x 63.5 cm
L.A. Louver Gallery, Venice, California

12. Wallace Berman
Semina suitcase c.1960
metal suitcase with collaged photographs
20.3 x 25.4 x 9.6 cm
Shirley Berman, Los Angeles: Courtesy L.A Louver Gallery, Venice, California

13. Wallace Berman
Facsimile journals to accompany Semina suitcase 1955-64
offset lithograph & letterpress printing on paper, boxed set of 9 volumes
30.7 x 25.7 x 5 cm
L.A. Louver Gallery, Venice, California

14. Wallace Berman
Untitled 1973
mixed media box with rock
24.1 x 24.1 x 15.2 cm
Mrs. Ann Janss

15. Joseph Beuys
Intuition . . . instead of a cookbook 1968
wooden box with pencil drawing
30 x 21 x 5 cm
Arts Council Collection, South Bank Centre, London

16. Joseph Beuys
Bruno Cora Tea 1975
bottle & herb tea, leaded top, printed label in glazed wood box
28.5 x 11 x 10.5 cm
Ronald Feldman Fine Arts, New York

17. Marinus Boezem
Della Scultura e La Luce 1985
mixed media
65 (diameter) x 9 cm
Rijksdienst Beeldende Kunst, Holland

18. Angel Bofarull
Untitled 1990
mixed media
5.5 x 7 x 8 cm
The artist

19. Derek Boshier
Marshal 1961
mixed media in box
50.8 x 40.6 x 10.1 cm
Brian Rice Collection

20. George Brecht
Games and Puzzle: Swim Puzzle 1965
plastic box containing dice & printed card
9.2 x 11.8 x 10 cm
Galerie 1900-2000, Marcel Fleiss, Paris

21. George Brecht
Water Yam (events) 1959-66
printed cards in plastic box
13 x 18 x 3 cm
Arts Council Collection, South Bank Centre, London

22. George Brecht
Deck A Flux Game 1966
plastic box & playing cards
6.7 x 9.3 x 2.3 cm
The Gilbert and Lila Silverman Fluxus
Collection, Detroit

23. George Brecht
*Games and Puzzles/Name Kit
1965-77*
mixed media in plastic box
9.3 x 12 x 1.8 cm
The Gilbert and Lila Silverman Fluxus
Collection, Detroit

24. George Brecht
Universal Machine II 1976
wooden box containing printed
paper & miscellaneous objects
28.3 x 28.3 x 4.1 cm
The Gilbert and Lila Silverman Fluxus
Collection, Detroit

25. George Brecht
*Valoche/A Flux Travel Aid
1975-78*
wooden box containing
miscellaneous objects
17.1 x 27.6 x 14.3 cm
The Gilbert and Lila Silverman Fluxus
Collection, Detroit

26. Marcel Broodthaers**
*I Return to Matter, I Rediscover
the Tradition of the Primitives,
Painting with Egg, Painting
with Egg 1966*
mixed media
25.7 x 25.7 x 7.6 cm
Trustees of the Tate Gallery

27. Marcel Broodthaers
*Treasure Island (L'Astragalus)
1974*
tin box, photograph, coin
14.6 x 10 x 3 cm
Marian Goodman, New York

28. Marcel Broodthaers
Untitled 1974
coronation souvenir tin of
Queen Elizabeth II, open tin
can with wire wool
14.5 x 12.3 x 10.8 cm
& 20 x 15 x 10 cm
Private collection

29. Marcel Broodthaers**
*Box with checkerboard design
& letters of the alphabet 1975*
wood, paper, painting
21 x 24.5 x 5 cm
Private collection

30. Jim Buckley
Colony 1990
plywood, lead, brass, interior
light & push button light switch
16 x 44 x 44 cm
The artist

31. Jim Buckley
Hasp 1990
galvanised steel, lead, plywood
& pop rivets
34 x 23 x 15 cm
The artist

32. James Burbidge
Echo 1991
wood, resin, bitumen/rubber
compound, treated lead foil,
lead sheet, papier mâché,
paint & glass
30.8 x 53.2 x 21.6 cm
Private collection, England & Co.
Gallery, London

33. James Burbidge
Warm 1992
MDF, glass, treated lead foil,
beeswax
36 x 66.3 x 23.3 cm
England & Co. Gallery, London

34. César
Container Expansion 1969
printed label, tin containing
polyurethane/Freon mixture
& pigment
17 x 10 cm in diameter
The artist

35. César
Match Combustion 1971
burnt matches & matchbox
on paper
70 x 40 cm
Collection Ferrero, Nice

36. César
Compression 1975
crushed carboard boxes
40 x 20 x 20 cm
The artist

37. César
Homage to the Teapot c.1976
wood box, plaster, hair & mask
26 x 7 x 5.5 cm
Collection Ferrero, Nice

38. John Chick
*Flux Food (forest and synthetic)
1968*
mixed media in plastic box
9.3 x 12 x 2.6 cm each
The Gilbert and Lila Silverman Fluxus
Collection, Detroit

39. William Christenberry
The Alabama Box 1980
mixed media
15.5 x 45 x 31.4 cm
The artist

40. William Christenberry
Klan Dolls 1992
mixed media
10.1 x 67.3 x 47 cm
The artist

41. Joseph Cornell
Untitled c.1945
box construction
24.1 x 14.6 x 9.5 cm
The Joseph and Robert Cornell
Memorial Foundation

42. Joseph Cornell**
Guiditta Pasta (Dedicace) 1950
mixed media
30.5 x 45.7 x 10.2 cm
Trustees of the Tate Gallery

43. Joseph Cornell
Untitled c. early 1950s
box construction
5 x 45.7 x 22.8 cm
The Joseph and Robert Cornell
Memorial Foundation

44. Joseph Cornell
Untitled c.1948-54
box construction
43.2 x 29.8 x 15.2 cm
The Joseph and Robert Cornell
Memorial Foundation

45. Joseph Cornell
Apollinaires 1954
box construction
43.2 x 30.5 x 14 cm
The Joseph and Robert Cornell
Memorial Foundation

46. Joseph Cornell
*L'Humeur Vagabonde
c. late 1950s*
box construction
17.2 x 19 x 8.2 cm
The Joseph and Robert Cornell
Memorial Foundation

47. Joseph Cornell
Untitled n.d.
box construction
47.6 x 31.2 x 12 cm
The Joseph and Robert Cornell
Memorial Foundation

48. Jeffrey Dennis
Six Easy Breathers 1991
oil paint on polymerised board
& canvas
150 x 100 x 170 cm
The artist

49. Steve Dilworth
The Fish Box 1991
driftwood, fish, fishing line,
bog oak
25 x 50 cm
Scottish Arts Council Collection

50. Marcel Duchamp***
The Green Box 1934
94 documents in a cardboard
box covered with flock paper
33 x 28 x 1.9 cm
Private collection

51. Marcel Duchamp***
Boîte en Valise (Series C) 1941
linen covered box, lined with
grey-blue Ingres paper
containing 68 items
9 x 38 x 40 cm
Private collection

52. Anthony Earnshaw
The Black Market 1988
mixed media
44 x 37 x 8 cm
The artist

53. Anthony Earnshaw
The Blind Engine Driver 1989
mixed media
25 x 60 x 11 cm
The artist

54. Anthony Earnshaw
*The Bride with Her Bachelors,
Again: after Marcel Duchamp
1991*
mixed media
44 x 40 x 10 cm
The artist

55. Yolande Fièvre
Untitled 18 March 1962
box relief with wood & stones
65 x 125 x 15 cm
Galerie Natalie Seroussi, Paris

56. Yolande Fièvre
Refuge pour le Rêve 1968
box relief with wood & stones
35 x 35 x 12 cm
Galerie Natalie Seroussi, Paris

57. Robert Filliou
Flux Hair c.1966
plastic box with hair
12 x 9.3 x 1.3 cm
The Gilbert and Lila Silverman Fluxus
Collection, Detroit

58. Robert Filliou
Optimistic box No. 1 1968
wooden box plus stone
11 x 11 x 11 cm
Arts Council Collection, South Bank
Centre, London

59. Robert Filliou
*Optimistic box No. 3: So much
better if you can't play chess
1968-70*
chessboard with two labels,
glued to both interior & exterior
12 x 6 x 3 cm
Galerie 1900-2000, Marcel Fleiss, Paris

60. Fluxus Collective
Flux Kit (BA copy) 1965
black vinyl attaché case
containing miscellaneous
boxed kits
32.5 x 44.5 x 12.5 cm (closed)
The Gilbert and Lila Silverman Fluxus
Collection, Detroit

61. Fluxus Collective
Fluxus Year Box 2 1966-68
wooden box containing
miscellaneous objects
20.3 x 20.3 x 8.6 cm
The Gilbert and Lila Silverman Fluxus
Collection, Detroit

62. Richard Hamilton
The Critic Laughs 1968-71
electric toothbrush, false teeth
& container
26.5 x 11 x 6 cm
The artist

63. Jann Haworth
Richard III 1980
wood, mirror, porcelain & paint
26.8 x 37 x 27.2 cm
Arts Council Collection, South Bank
Centre, London

64. Geoffrey Hendricks
Flux Reliquary 1973
plastic box, printed card &
miscellaneous objects
12 x 9.2 x 2.3 cm
The Gilbert and Lila Silverman Fluxus
Collection, Detroit

65. Maurice Henry
The Little Arsonist 1965
matches, lighter, paper,
woodwool, straw, matchwood,
petrol & instructions
28 x 28 x 4 cm
Arts Council Collection, South Bank
Centre, London

66. Maurice Henry
Homage to Paganini 1968
wood, straw & cloth
53 x 26 x 12 cm
Arts Council Collection, South Bank
Centre, London

67. George Herms
Drugstore for Artie 1991-92
mixed media
269.2 x 259 x 91.4 cm
The artist and L.A. Louver Gallery,
Venice, California

68. Susan Hiller
Nama-Ma (Mother) 1991
Australian native earths, rouge
containers & photocopy
25.4 x 34.2 x 6.35 cm
Gimpel Fils, London

69. Susan Hiller
*Chamin-Ha (House of Knives)
1992*
obsidian projectile points &
photocopy
25.4 x 34.2 x 6.35 cm
Gimpel Fils, London

70. Susan Hiller
Sophia (Wisdom) 1993
antique bottles, four waters,
labels, photocopy & wax
25.4 x 34.2 x 6.35 cm
Gimpel Fils, London

71. Rebecca Horn
*Love Affair Between a Goose
Egg and a Brown Paper Bag
1990*
glass, steel vitrine, music sheets,
goose egg, paper bag
102.8 x 69.8 x 35.5 cm
Margulies Family Collection

72. Georges Hugnet**
Untitled c.1936-37
box with model sailing ship, dice
& collage of women's faces
11.5 x 17 x 4 cm
Timothy Baum, New York

73. Joe Jones
Fluxmusic c.1965
black vinyl attaché case
containing 10 winding devices
32.5 x 44.5 x 12.5 cm
The Gilbert and Lila Silverman Fluxus
Collection, Detroit

74. Per Kirkeby
*Solid Plastic in Plastic Box
1967*
12 x 9.4 x 1.1 cm
The Gilbert and Lila Silverman Fluxus
Collection, Detroit

75. Jiří Kolář
Nest Box 1974
chiasmage on wooden nest box
108.6 x 72.5 x 75 cm
Musée National d'Art Moderne, Centre
Georges Pompidou, Paris

76. Françoise Lacampagne
*Energie Dissipative (Homage to
Yves Klein) 1990*
wood, stone & pigment
each part 63 x 38 x 21 cm
J.P. Ledeur, Paris

77. Françoise Lacampagne
Souffle (Breath) 1993
wood, pebbles & brick
47 x 16 x 12 cm
Private collection, Paris

78. Nikolaus Lang
Untitled c.1970
mixed media assemblage in
perspex box
16.3 x 12.1 x 5.6 cm
Penrose Collection, England

79. Sol LeWitt
Light Cube 1961-62
painted wood, photograph
& lightbulb
39 x 30 x 30 cm
Galerie 1900-2000, Marcel Fleiss, Paris
and Pierre Huber, Geneva

80. George Maciunas
New Flux Year c.1967
box containing pop-out snake
12 x 17 x 7 cm
The Gilbert and Lila Silverman Fluxus
Collection, Detroit

81. George Maciunas*****
Flux Smile Machine 1972
blue opaque plastic box
containing spring loaded device
12 x 9.3 x 3.3 cm
Tate Gallery Archives

82. Will Maclean
Fladday Reliquary 1978
found objects, bird & bone
55 x 43 x 10 cm
Inverness Museum and Art Gallery

83. Will Maclean
China Nights 1983
painted wood & mirrors
102 x 71.4 x 16 cm
Glasgow Art Gallery and Museum

84. Man Ray
Mr. Knife and Miss Fork 1944
assemblage of wood, metal,
string & tissue
33.8 x 22.8 x 3.7 cm
Lucien Treillard Collection

85. Man Ray
Letter Box 1965
Metal letter box filled with
plaster letters on white
formica mount
28 x 14.2 x 5.4 cm
Timothy Baum, New York

86. Man Ray
Lips of Gold (Lèvres d'Or) 1967
mixed media
5.2 x 26 x 38.4 cm
Zabriskie Gallery, New York

87. Man Ray
The Pear of Erik Satie 1969
assemblage of painted wood
& plastic
36.5 x 24 x 11.5 cm
Lucien Treillard Collection

88. Man Ray
Pechage 1969
assemblage with painted wood
box & plastic
36 x 24 x 11.5 cm
Lucien Treillard Collection

89. Man Ray
Voilà 1970-73
assemblage with painted wood
& canvas, & paintbrush
35 x 22 x 20.8 cm
Lucien Treillard Collection

90. Marcel Mariën
The School of Voyeurs 1971
glass fronted box incorporating
small objects
26.8 x 65.1 x 24.5 cm
Private collection, London

91. Larry Miller
Sunflower 1985
satin-lined box containing dead
sunflower
55.5 x 39 cm
Henry Buhl, New York

92. Robert Morris
Untitled 1963
paint on wood, metal
& padlock
28 x 20 x 9 cm.
Sonnabend Collection

93. Charles Murray
Snuff Box 1950
mahogany, oil, pen & ink, brass
nails, inlay & cork
5 x 3.8 x 10.7 cm
Andrew Murray

94. Louise Nevelson****
Large Cryptic II 1969
painted wood & metal hinges
box: 24.1 x 38.1 x 27.3 cm;
stick: 22.2 x 0.6 cm
Whitney Museum of American Art:
Gift of the Pace Gallery 70.1577 a-b

95. Louise Nevelson****
Night-Focus-Dawn 1969
24 painted wood boxes on base
259.1 x 297.2 x 35.6 cm
Whitney Museum of American Art:
Purchased with funds from Howard
and Jean Lipman 69.73

96. Avis Newman
Object From Nature 1986
two bird skulls, frottage from
floorboards on japanese paper
& linen
36.5 x 21.5 x 9 cm
Lisson Gallery, London

97. Avis Newman
*Cyphers Which Supply A Place
But Signify Nothing 1990*
box with wax, snail shells
& plastic
23 x 9.8 x 5.3 cm
Lisson Gallery, London

98. Avis Newman
*Bird Box: La Scatola
dell'Uccello 1992*
wood, glass, steel
98 x 73 x 13.5 cm
Arts Council Collection, South Bank
Centre, London

99. Claes Oldenburg
London Knees 1966-68
cast latex painted with
coloured polyurethane, felt,
cast acrylic, 21 offset
lithographs on paper in cloth
covered travelling case
27 x 41 x 39 cm
Arts Council Collection, South Bank
Centre, London

100. Claes Oldenburg
*Double Nose/Purse/Punching
Bag/Ashtray 1970*
leather, bronze, wood, metal
& bark chips
21.3 x 52.7 x 27.6 cm
Gemini Editions, Los Angeles

101. Yoko Ono
All White Chess Set 1962-70
acrylic on wood
3.4 x 17.1 x 12.7 cm
Arts Council Collection, South Bank
Centre, London

102. Meret Oppenheim
Box with Little Animals 1963
small box with sliding cover,
interior painted in oil, Italian
bowtie pasta
15 x 27 x 18 cm
Private collection

103. Meret Oppenheim
The Cocoon (It's Alive) 1974
box of wood with cover of
plexiglass, cushion of satin
with filling of mercury
& branches
9 x 16 x 13 cm
Birgit and Burkhard Wenger, Basel

104. Mimi Parent
Eve Rêve 1973
mixed media
92.7 x 62.2 x 14 cm
Danielle Boile Collection, France

105. Attributed to
Roland Penrose
Untitled 1946-50
oil paint inside perspex box
8.2 x 12.7 x 1.7 cm
Private collection, on loan to the
Penrose Collection, England

106. Robert Rauschenberg
*Untitled (Scatole Personali
series) c.1952*
painted wood box with twig
beetle
3.8 x 7.6 x 5.3cm
The artist

107. Robert Rauschenberg
*Music Box (Elemental
Sculpture) 1953*
wood, nails, 3 pebbles &
feather
30 x 19.6 x 23.5 cm
Jasper Johns Collection

108. Patrick Raynaud***
*Fantin-Latour's Suitcase:
Homage to Delacroix 1989*
illuminated cibachrome
photographs & flight cases
170 x 62 x 60 cm each (closed)
The artist

109. Patrick Raynaud
*Cousin's suitcase, Eva Prima
Pandora 1990*
illuminated cibachrome
photograph & flight case
70 x 150 x 50 cm (closed)
The artist

110. Martial Raysse
Nécropolis II 1960
objects in perspex boxes
68 x 20 x 20 cm
Private collection, Sweden. Courtesy of
Galerie Bonnier, Geneva

111. Florence Régnier-Barral
*Untitled 1989 (from the series
Places)*
plaster, wood, mosaic & sand
40 x 99.5 x 13 cm
The artist

112. Florence Régnier-Barral
*Untitled 1989 (from the series
Inside Out)*
wood, plaster, mirrors
& pigment
63 x 63 x 17 cm
The artist

113. James Riddle
Flux Clock Cabinet 1966
25 clockfaces, 1 clock, 1 cabinet
circa 38 x 38 x 38 cm
The Gilbert and Lila Silverman Fluxus
Collection, Detroit

114. James Riddle
E.S.P. Fluxkit 1966-68
plastic box containing different
coloured cards
9.2 x 11.8 x 0.8 cm
Galerie 1900-2000, Marcel Fleiss, Paris

115. Larry Rivers
Webster and Cigars 1962
mixed media & collage
on wood
32.7 x 40.6 x 40 cm
The artist

116. Takako Saito*****
*Flux Chess: Grinder Chess
c.1965-70*
wooden box containing
28 chess pieces (blue &
white buffer brushes &
grinding stones)
17 x 17 x 7.4 cm
Tate Gallery Archives

117. Lucas Samaras
Box No. 32 1965
wood, artificial hair & bones
33 x 25.4 x 38.1 cm
Saatchi Collection, London

118. Lucas Samaras
Box No. 51 1966
light bulbs, coloured yarn
& painted wood
35.5 x 37.4 x 35.5 cm
Saatchi Collection, London

119. Lucas Samaras**
Room No.3 1968
mirror on wood frame
274.3 x 274.3 x 274.3 cm
Saatchi Collection, London

120. Lucas Samaras
Untitled late 1960s
box containing sea coral, cotton
wool with pins & yarn
16.5 x 30.5 x 21 cm
The Mayor Gallery

121. Kurt Schwitters*
'3' 1922
inlaid wooden box
6.8 x 16.7 x 9.4 cm
Marlborough International Fine Art

122. Kurt Schwitters
*To Roland Peppenrose 5 April
1940*
pencil drawing on opened-out
cigarette box
7.3 x 14.6 cm
Private collection
Courtesy of The Mayor Gallery

123. Daniel Spoerri
Vera's Sewing Kit 1960
mixed media
8 x 23 x 15 cm
Sonnabend Collection

124. Daniel Spoerri
*Fake Arman by Spoerri
"real fleas" April 1976*
pencil case with accumulated
pen nibs glued to interior
8 x 21.4 x 2.7 cm
Galerie 1900-2000, Marcel Fleiss, Paris

125. Fred Stiven
Dark Box 1975
mixed media
27 x 15 x 10 cm
The artist

126. Fred Stiven
Margin Box 1991
mixed media
43 x 43 x 8 cm
The artist

127. Ben Vautier
Total art matchbox 1965
matchbox with printed label
& matches
3.5 x 5.1 x 1.3 cm.
The Gilbert and Lila Silverman Fluxus
Collection, Detroit

128. Ben Vautier
*Flux Box Containing God
c.1966*
plastic box
9.3 x 12 x 1.6 cm
The Gilbert and Lila Silverman Fluxus
Collection, Detroit

129. Ben Vautier
Suicide Kit 1967
various items in plastic box
14 x 10 x 2 cm
Arts Council Collection, South Bank
Centre, London

130. Paule Vézelay
Lines in Space No.3 1936
painted canvas & string
58.5 x 50 x 7 cm
Estate of Paule Vezelay, England & Co.
Gallery, London

131. Paule Vézelay
Lines in Space No 56 1969
painted wood & string
50 x 54.5 x 11 cm
Estate of Paule Vezelay, England & Co.
Gallery, London

132. Robert Watts
Art Rat Box No. 2 1973
box containing walnut shells
placed on steel pins
36 x 24 x 7 cm
Galerie 1900-2000, Marcel Fleiss, Paris

133. Robert Watts
Flux Atlas 1973
plastic box containing stones
& printed cards
21.2 x 32.7 x 5.7 cm
The Gilbert and Lila Silverman Fluxus
Collection, Detroit

134. Huang Yongping
*The history of Chinese art and
the history of modern Western
art washed in a washing
machine for two minutes 1987*
(this version re-made 1993)
mixed media
80 x 50 x 50 cm
The artist

135. Johanes Zechner
A Boy 1993
acrylic, household paint &
collage òn chipboard coffin
251 x 178 x 6 cm
Francis Graham-Dixon Gallery, London

136. Johanes Zechner***
Gepäck! The Big Issue 1993
acrylic paint & collage
on canvas (17 pieces) for
a suitcase
circa 325 x 380 cm
Schömer Collection, Klosterneuburg,
Austria

137. Krystyna Ziach
Memory of Rain 1993
wood box, mirror & photograph
41 x 48 x 6 cm
Private collection

95

127. Ben Vautier
Total art matchbox 1965
matchbox with printed label
& matches
3.5 x 5.1 x 1.3 cm.
The Gilbert and Lila Silverman Fluxus
Collection, Detroit
© ADAGP, Paris & DACS, London 1994

Exhibition organised by Alexandra Noble and Cindy Hubert

Catalogue designed by Edwin Belchamber
Edited by Linda Schofield
Typeset by Wayzgoose Phototypesetting
Printed by Amica Fine Art Print Ltd

Photographic Credits
Catalogue numbers: 4, 23, 38, 57, 60, 61, 64, 73, 116, 128, 133, Brad
Iverson; 44, 45, 46, Bill Jacobson, Courtesy of Pace Gallery, New York;
75, Philippe Migeat; 79, Art and Public, Geneva; 80, Buzz Silverman;
113, George Maciunas; 127, Eric Silverman.

ISBN 1 85332 128 1

A full list of Arts Council and South Bank Centre publications may be
obtained from: Publications, The South Bank Centre, Royal Festival Hall,
London SE1 8XX

THE
SOUTH
BANK
CENTRE

Cover image:
44. Joseph Cornell,
Untitled c. 1948-54
box construction
43.2 x 29.8 x 15.2 cm
The Joseph and Robert Cornell
Memorial Foundation